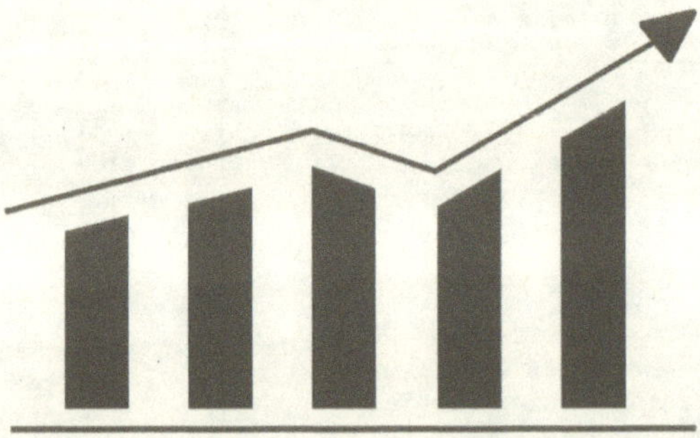

Year of Publication: 2026
Publisher: Fame Finders Media
₹ 599/-

Head Office:
8A/8, WEA, Karol Bagh, New Delhi – 110005

Email: info@famefinders.in
Website: www.famefinders.in

DEDICATION

This book is dedicated to the loving memory of my beloved grandmother, whose blessings, affection, and silent love continue to illuminate every step of my life.

"Though you are no longer here, you remain the source of every inspiration."

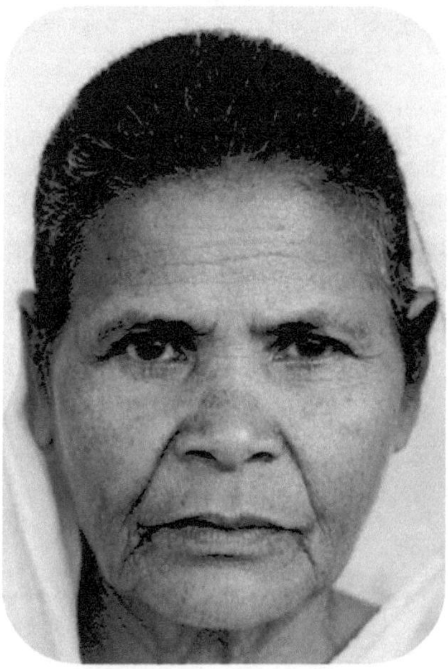

Bholanath Das

(In loving memory of my beloved grandmother Bholanath Das, whose blessings continue to guide every step of my journey.)

INTRODUCTION

To many people, the stock market seems like a complex and frightening place. Price fluctuations, uncertainty, and risk make it appear as though it is designed only for experts. But the truth is different—the market itself is never truly complicated; rather, the way we try to understand it often makes it seem complicated.

This book is written to change that perspective. Here, we will try to view the market in a new way—not merely through charts or patterns, but through the stories hidden behind them. Usually, we only notice price movements, while ignoring the thoughts, emotions, and decisions of people that actually drive those movements.

Gradually, you will realize that the stock market is not just about numbers or graphs; it is a behavioral system. Fear, greed, hope, and patience together shape the direction of the market. Once you begin to understand these behaviors, your ability to make decisions becomes much stronger.

The purpose of this book is not to confine you within rigid rules or strategies. Rather, it aims to help you build a mindset through which you can make sound decisions based on your own observations and experiences. The true objective of learning here is not merely understanding *what happens*, but realizing *why it happens*.

When you understand the market at this level, trading no longer remains only a technical process—it becomes a discipline of the mind and emotions. And this discipline is what ultimately helps you achieve long-term success.
In the end, the goal of this book is not only to make you a better trader, but also a more aware and capable decision-maker.

BOOK DESCRIPTION

"The Hidden Psychology Of the Stock Market"

This is not an ordinary trading guide. It is a journey—one that seeks to understand the market not only through charts and numbers, but also through human psychology, behavior, and decision-making.

In this book, you will find:

- Deep analysis of index and market behavior
- Option trading and real market thinking
- Practical application of patterns
- The impact of VIX, global markets, and the economy
- And most importantly—the correct way to make decisions

the primary purpose of this book is to prepare you in such a way that you do not merely trade, but truly understand the market and make decisions with confidence.

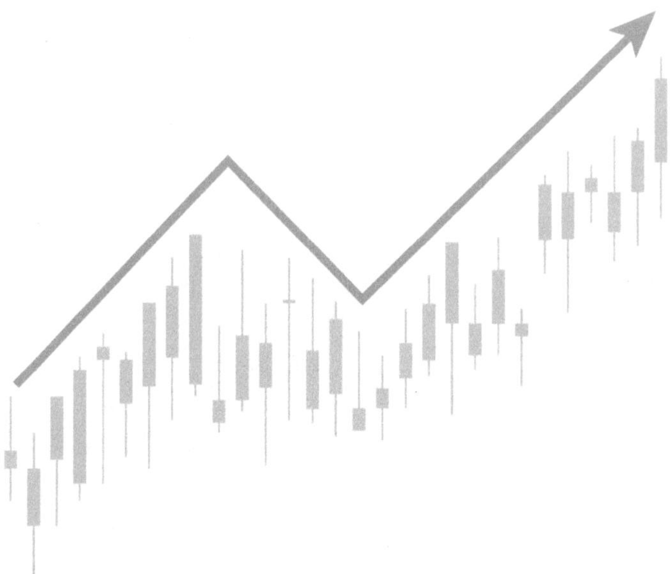

FOREWORD

To many, the stock market is simply a place for profit; to others, it is a place of fear and uncertainty. But for those who truly understand it, the market is a field of learning—one that teaches something new every day.

Through this book, Bholanath Das presents a different perspective, where trading is not merely a strategy, but a way of thinking. This book will not only provide readers with information, but also teach them how to think.

I believe this book will be equally valuable for both beginners and experienced readers alike.

ACKNOWLEDGMENTS

This book would not have been possible alone.
First of all, I am grateful to my family and loved ones, whose support and patience have always helped me move forward.

My heartfelt thanks to my students, because their questions, mistakes, and eagerness to learn have constantly inspired me to think in new ways.
I am also grateful to all those people who have directly or indirectly stood beside me throughout this journey.

Finally, I dedicate this book to the memory of my beloved grandmother, Bholanath Das, whose blessings continue to light my path even today.

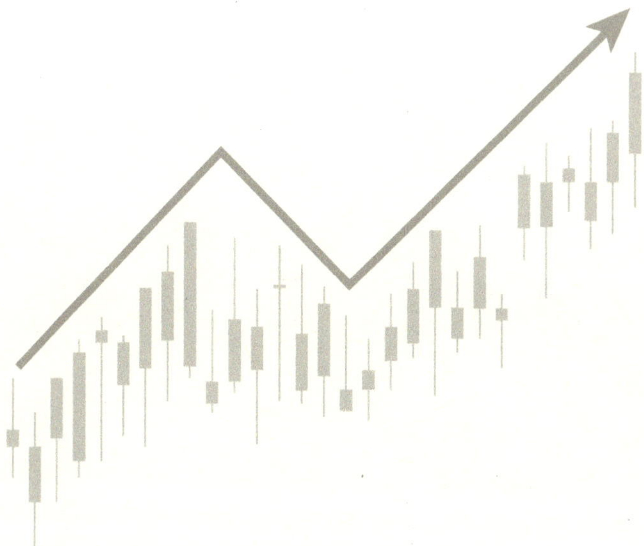

PROLOGUE

For many people, the first encounter with the market is confusing.

Some make profits, some suffer losses—but very few truly understand why this difference exists.
This book is an attempt to search for that "why."
There are no shortcuts here, no secret formulas.

There is only observation, experience, and a different path of thinking.

If you read this book with attention and sincerity, perhaps you will begin to see the market in a completely new way.

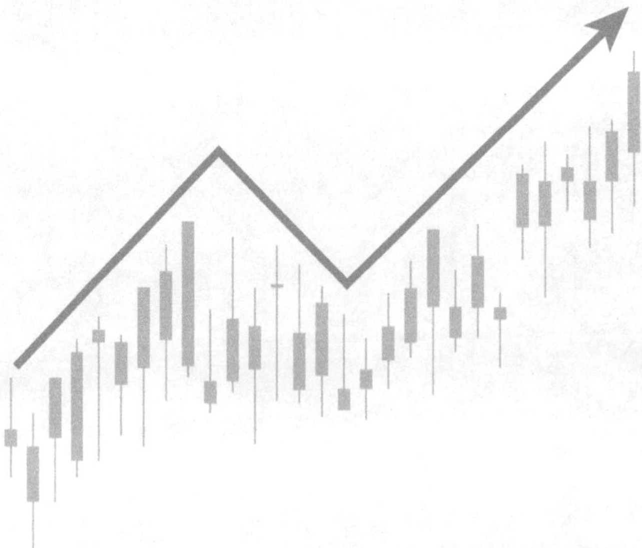

AUTHOR'S MESSAGE

This book is not written merely to teach the stock market; it is written to help you understand the market in a new way. Many times, we depend heavily on charts, patterns, or signals, yet the true power of the market lies hidden in human behavior, fear, hope, and decision-making.

From my experience, I have seen that successful traders do not always know more information—they simply know how to think correctly. Every chapter of this book is designed to help build that perspective, where you will not only understand *what is happening*, but also *why it is happening*.

I do not want you to blindly follow any fixed rule after reading this book. Rather, I want you to gradually build your own decision-making ability through observation, experience, and judgment.

Making profits in the market is important, but even more important are patience, control, and consistency. Remember—the market never rushes, but those who rush rarely survive in it for long.

If this book can bring even a small change to your way of thinking, then my effort will be successful.

— Bholanath Das

AUTHOR INTRODUCTION

Bholanath Das is an educator, researcher, and social worker honored with the *National Lal Bahadur Shastri Award*. He has received numerous recognitions across the country for his remarkable contributions to education and social service.

He is currently serving as the Head of Institution at **Phulbari Sitala High School (H.S.)**, located in the Gangasagar region of Sundarban, South 24 Parganas.

Having been born and raised in the remote island region of the Sundarbans, he deeply understands the realities of rural life. Those experiences have profoundly influenced his values, thoughts, and sense of social responsibility.

Professionally, he is a teacher as well as an **SEBI Certified Expert, NISM certified Research Analyst & Research Head & Educator.**

Drawing from his long experience in India's financial markets, he combines market psychology, behavioral economics, and practical trading experience to present complex financial concepts in a simple, understandable, and inspiring manner for ordinary readers.

He is associated with the **School of Day Traders** as a Research Head and Mentor, working continuously in the field of stock market education and promoting financial awareness among ordinary people.

His research-based tool, **SODT Swing Master Premium,** has already gained popularity among many traders and investors, giving him a distinct identity in this field.

He is also well known as a **TEDx Speaker**.
As a teacher—discipline,
As a researcher—curiosity,
And as a social worker—a sense of humanity and responsibility—

These three core values form the foundation of his philosophy, thinking, and outlook on life.

His work, "The Hidden Psychology Of the Stock Market", is not merely a book about the stock market; it is a sincere exploration of the deep connection between markets, human psychology, society, and the realities of life.

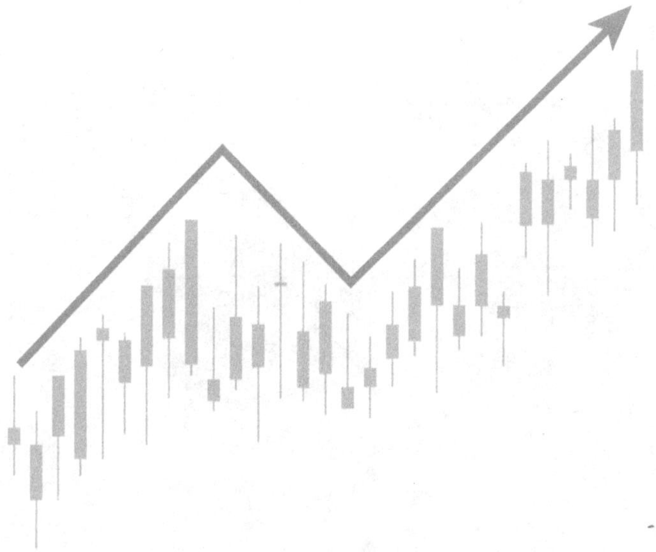

-1.68%
72.67
+4.37%
380.44
259
125

MESSAGE OF BEST WISHES

It gives me immense pleasure to extend my heartfelt congratulations to Mr. Bholanath Das on the publication of his insightful book on the stock market. This work reflects not only his deep knowledge and expertise but also his commitment to educating and empowering individuals in the field of financial literacy.

In today's rapidly evolving economic landscape, understanding the stock market is no longer a luxury but a necessity. This book, with its simplified approach to technical and options analysis, serves as a valuable guide for both beginners and experienced investors. It has the potential to inspire readers to make informed decisions and build confidence in navigating financial markets.

I commend Mr. Das for his dedication and contribution to spreading practical knowledge in such an important domain. His efforts will undoubtedly benefit countless readers and aspiring traders.

I wish this book great success and hope it reaches a wide audience across the globe.

With best wishes,
Prof. Dr. Parin Somani
Director
London Organisation of Skills Development
London, United Kingdom

MESSAGE OF APPRECIATION

Dear Das, Bholanath

It is with great pleasure that I extend my heartfelt wishes to Bholanath Das on the release of his insightful book on the stock market. This work beautifully simplifies the complexities of trading and investing, making it accessible to learners from all walks of life.

In a world where financial literacy is more important than ever, this book stands as a guiding light—empowering individuals to understand markets not just as numbers, but as stories of discipline, strategy, and vision. Bholanath Das has combined knowledge with clarity, offering readers both confidence and direction.

I truly believe this book will inspire aspiring traders, investors, and young minds to approach the financial world with curiosity and courage. May it reach countless readers and create a positive impact in their journey toward financial independence.

Wishing you continued success and global recognition for your valuable contribution.

With warm regards,
Dame Munni Irone
Founder, Art 4 Peace Awards
Philanthropist & Corporate Trainer
Beverly Hills, CA, USA

MESSAGE OF APPRECIATION

I extend my heartfelt congratulations and best wishes to my former colleague and distinguished educator, Mr. Bholanath Das, on the publication of his valuable book, *"The Hidden Psychology Of the Stock Market."*

I firmly believe that this book will inspire countless readers and play an important role in increasing financial awareness. In my opinion, the author has successfully presented complex stock market concepts in a simple, clear, and elegant manner, making the book equally beneficial for both beginners and experienced readers.

As a teacher, researcher, and social worker, his dedication and vision are reflected throughout every page of this work. I feel proud of his remarkable achievement and sincerely wish him greater success and creative accomplishments in the future.

— Anirban Chakraborty

MESSAGE OF APPRECIATION

I feel extremely happy and proud to know that our respected Head Teacher, Mr. Bholanath Das, is publishing his book on the stock market titled *"A Story Seen From Within."* I extend my heartfelt congratulations and best wishes to him for this important achievement.

I hope this book will play a significant role in increasing financial awareness among people from all sections of society—from ordinary individuals to middle-class and upper-class readers alike. I also believe that readers will warmly appreciate this valuable work.

I sincerely wish that his efforts continue to achieve even greater success in the future.

Samir Majhi
Assistant Teacher
Phulbari Sitala High School (H. S.)

MESSAGE OF APPRECIATION

Book Publication

The phrase "Book Publication" beautifully reflects the sacred relationship between a teacher and a student. For a respected and talented individual, publishing a book is the very first step in expressing one's thoughts, ideas, and wisdom in the most refined and meaningful manner. Every author pours out their emotions, experiences, and knowledge for readers through their writings.

With such a unique vision of "Book Publication," respected Shri Bholanath Das began this remarkable initiative. Sir is a recipient of various national-level awards and has deeply explored the world of the stock market to gain profound knowledge and understanding, which inspired the creation of this book.

This is not a conventional book that teaches simple alphabets like A, B, C, D or basic lessons. Rather, this book serves as a pathway to success in life by absorbing its knowledge into every aspect of one's personality and existence.

Just as a drop of impure water shines brightly when it falls upon a lotus leaf, our SODT educational institution works in a similar way. Students from any background or level can gain knowledge from this institution and create opportunities to establish themselves successfully in society.

Respectful pranam to you, Sir. Stay blessed and healthy.

Devroy Ghosh
Student
School of Day Traders

MESSAGE OF APPRECIATION

In my eyes, the way Bholanath Das understands the Indian stock market is like Arjuna's focused vision toward the eye of the bird. I personally feel that very few people can observe and understand the market the way he does.

I believe that the creation of the SODT Strategy Master Premium is the result of immense hard work, concentration, persistence, failures, and ultimate success. As a small trader myself, I may never fully understand the level of dedication behind it, but I truly feel that this tool has become a powerful support system for many traders.

In today's world, where unemployment is becoming a serious issue, I believe his work has helped many people create financial opportunities for themselves. To me, this tool is not only meant for making profits through proper entries and exits, but also for protecting traders from wrong decisions and unnecessary losses.

I sincerely congratulate him on this wonderful addition to the world of stock market education. Even if I may never reach his level, I hope I can at least follow in his footsteps.

Finally, I pray that God always stands beside a person who dedicates himself to the welfare of society in such a selfless way.

Abhijit Sanyal
Student
School of Day Traders

MESSAGE OF APPRECIATION

From the depths of my heart, I express my respect to my beloved Sir.

Today is a very special day because Sir's book on the stock market is being published. Having the opportunity to learn from him has helped me think and understand many things in a completely new way. His guidance has created a clear path before us, where we are trying to move forward step by step.

To me, this book is not merely a publication; it is a reflection of Sir's experience and journey of learning. I believe readers will gain new perspectives and opportunities for growth through this work.

Sir is not only a teacher to us, but also someone who constantly inspires and motivates us on our learning journey.

I sincerely wish him success in this achievement and hope he continues to accomplish even greater things in the future.

Rahul Roy
Student
School of Day Traders

MESSAGE OF APPRECIATION

From the depths of my heart, I offer my respect to you, Sir.

Before I came to know you in the stock market journey, I was surrounded by uncertainty and had suffered losses because of several wrong decisions. Still, I continued trying to learn. At that time, getting the opportunity to learn from you became an important turning point in my life.

From you, I learned not only trading, but also patience, discipline, and the habit of thinking practically. By following your guidance and using your indicators, I am now able to trade with far more awareness and confidence than before.

My learning journey is still continuing, but gradually I am improving and hoping to do even better in the future.

Thank you, Sir. Your guidance is truly valuable to me.

Arijit Das
Student
School of Day Traders

TABLE OF CONTENTS

PART 1

The Mind of the Market

(Human Psychology and Market Movements)

CHAPTER 1

What is the Market?

The morning sunlight in the village had not yet fully risen. The school bell had not rung yet. I was sitting on the bench of a tea stall with a folded copy of the AAJKAL newspaper in my hand. Beside me sat Nitai-da—the man who seemed to know everything and talk about everything.

Steam was rising from the tea cups, and in the middle of the conversation, one word kept returning again and again—
"Market."

"Yesterday the shares fell badly in the market!" Nitai-da said with concern in his voice.

I smiled and asked,
"You know about shares too?"

He replied,
"No, but I hear that the people who understand them become rich overnight."

That was the first time the word sounded different to me—
"Market."

We go to markets every day—to buy vegetables, rice, and lentils. But this other market, where people buy "parts of companies" and sell "beliefs"—what kind of market is this?

From that day, a question began growing inside me—

"Why do people buy?"

"Why do they sell?"

"What is hidden behind this buying and selling?"

Later I realized—

The market is a reflection of the human mind.
On the days people are hopeful, prices rise.
On the days fear increases, prices fall.

That means the market is actually a collective mind, where the thoughts of millions merge together.

Just as a teacher can understand from students' faces who has studied and who has not, the market's every rise and fall tells the story hidden inside people.

Charts, lines, and candles

these are only external languages.

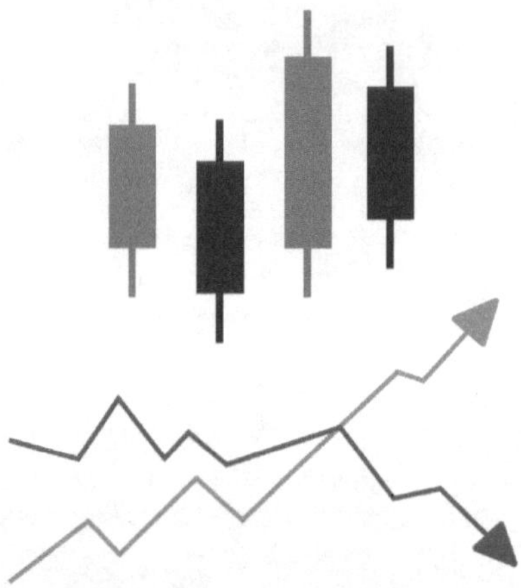

The real truth hidden inside is **psychology.**

At one time, I learned candlesticks, trendlines, and many technical methods. But the more I learned, the more I understood—

"You cannot understand the market only by looking at charts; once you understand the mind, the charts begin to speak."

Once I saw an elderly investor sitting quietly in the corner of an office. The market was crashing and everyone around him was panicking and selling.

I asked him,
"Sir, aren't you doing anything?"
He smiled and replied,
"I don't watch the market; I watch people."

That one sentence changed my life.

That day I understood—

The market is not about price; it is about belief.

The market is not about time; it is about patience.

The market is not about opportunity; it is about preparation.

Whether in a trading room, a broker's office, or sitting alone before a screen—the market is actually a reflection of ourselves.

The calmer we are, the clearer the market appears.
The more restless we are, the more confusing the market becomes.

Just as a teacher understands the emotional ups and downs of students every day, a trader also learns to understand the emotional movements of the market each day.

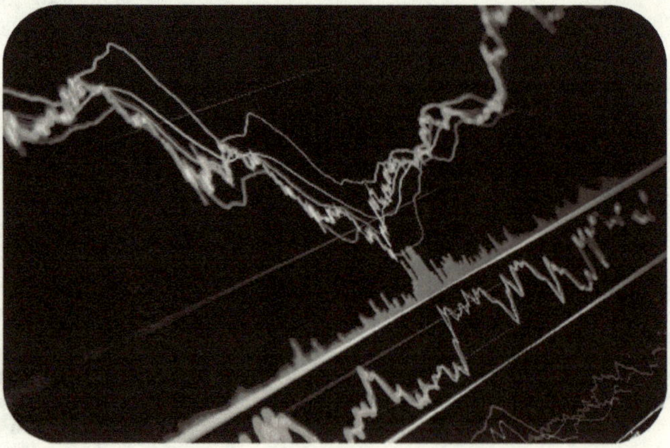

The only difference is this— Here, passing marks are not determined by scores, but by patience.

Summary

- The market is not about prices; it is about the human mind.
- Fear, greed, and hope together create the rhythm of the market.
- Charts contain truth, but psychology is the language of that truth.
- A trader is not merely a reader of charts, but a reader of people.

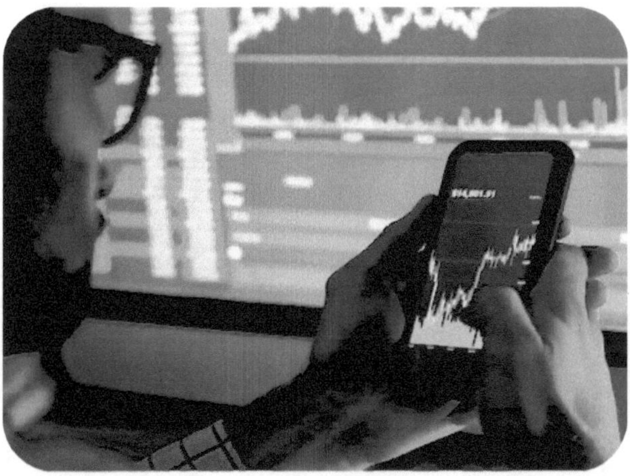

"The market does not teach how to earn money; it teaches how to become human."

— BHOLANATH DAS

CHAPTER 2

The Stage of Fear and Greed

The market day had begun very calmly.

The morning sunlight was soft and peaceful, and the Nifty chart also appeared flat and stable.

But suddenly, by afternoon, news arrived that a major company's earnings had declined.

Within minutes, prices started falling.

The screen that had been glowing green slowly turned red.

A question immediately arose in the mind—
"Should I sell everything?"
That is fear.

And this fear controls thousands of decisions every single day.

Fear teaches people to sell at the wrong time.

Greed teaches them to buy at the wrong time.

These two forces are the main actors on the grand stage of the market.
Opposite fear sits greed—
It whispers to people,
"Buy one more time... maybe this time the profit will double."
But the market teaches differently.

Here, punishment is fast, while rewards come slowly.
One young trader once told me,
"Sir, in just one week I turned 20,000 into 40,000!"
I smiled and replied,
"The speed at which money comes is often the speed at which it disappears."

To conquer fear and greed does not mean destroying them.

It means recognizing them, understanding them, and keeping a healthy distance from them.

Successful traders turn fear into a teacher and greed into a warning signal.

Summary

• Fear teaches caution, but decisions made purely from fear lead to losses.

• Greed inspires ambition, but excessive greed brings destruction.

• Success comes when the mind is balanced—not merely through indicators.

• Fear and greed are the language of the market; traders must learn to interpret them.

"Understanding fear does not mean seeing danger; it means recognizing opportunity."

— BHOLANATH DAS

CHAPTER 3

Trader vs Gambler

One evening, I saw a few men playing cards at a tea stall.
One of them said,
"This time luck is on my side."

There was excitement in their eyes, but also fear.
That scene felt exactly like the market.
Every day in the market, thousands of people think in the same way—
"Today luck is with me."

But the market does not move by luck; it moves through discipline.
A gambler thinks,
"Today my fortune is good, so I'll buy."

A trader thinks,
"My system is giving me a signal to buy."
The action may appear the same, but the thinking is completely different.
The trader who writes down and follows rules every day does not fight the market—he cooperates with it.

But the one who thinks, "Let's see what fate decides," loses not to the market, but to his own impatience and instability.

When I experienced my first major loss, I realized something important—
The market had not defeated me; I had defeated myself.
Because financial losses in the market are temporary,
but the loss of mental strength can become permanent.

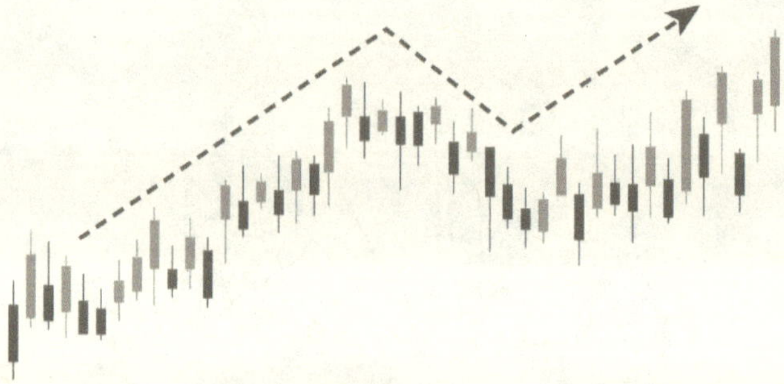

Summary

• The market itself is never gambling, but a person without discipline turns it into gambling.

• A gambler believes in luck; a trader believes in rules.

• "Not trading" is also a form of trading.

• True success is not conquering the market, but conquering self-control.

"The greatest victory in the market is not profit, but discipline."

— BHOLANATH DAS

CONCLUSION

"The market is actually a mirror where we see ourselves. Fear, greed, and hope—these are the very things through which people both lose and learn."

1.618
0.382
0.25
1.618
0.625
2.618
0.786
0.25
0.25
0.75
0.382

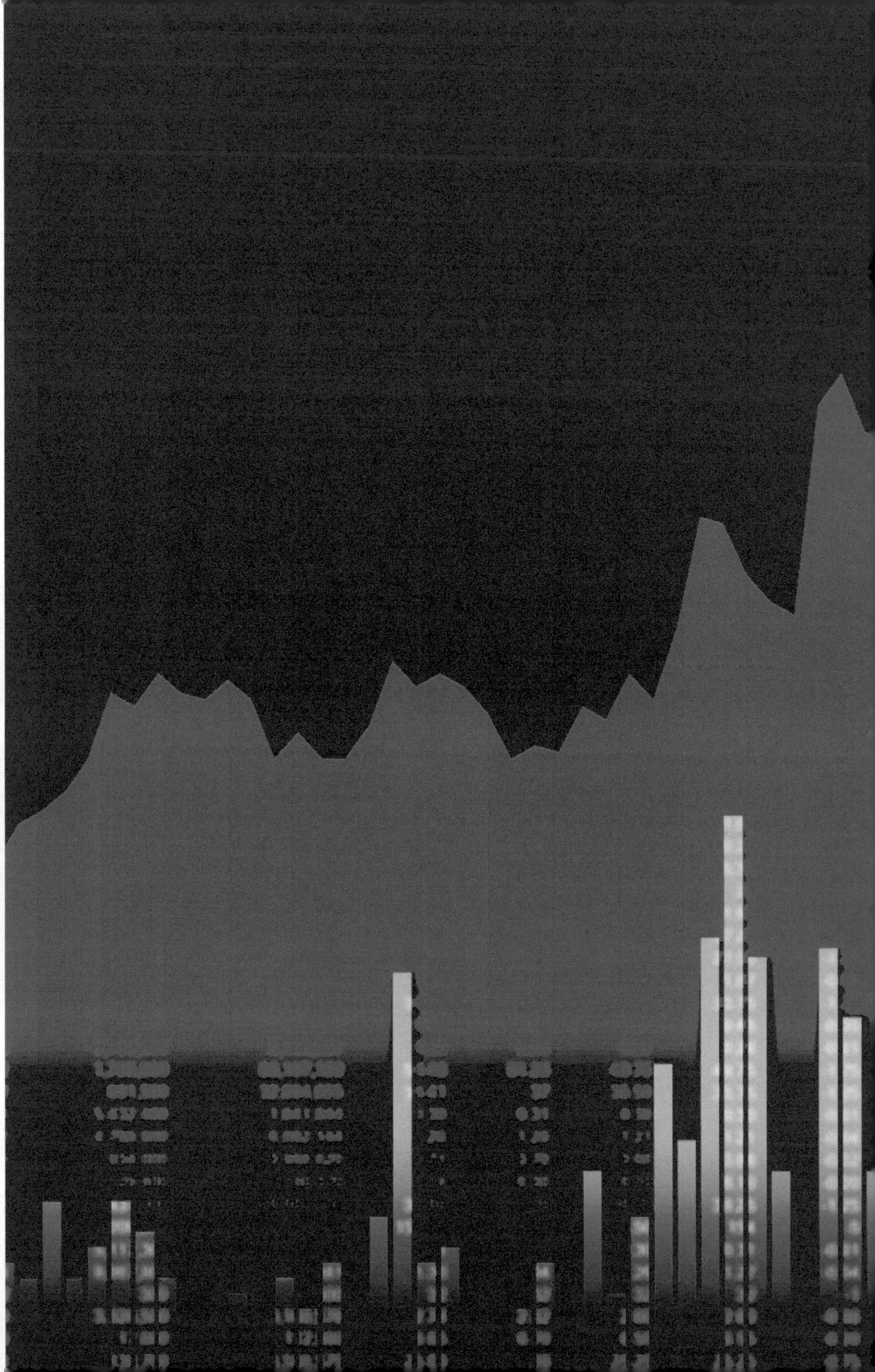

PART 2

Not Charts, But Character

Understanding the market is not about understanding lines, but understanding thought itself.

CHAPTER 4

The Story Behind the Chart

The first time I looked at a chart,
it felt like a mountain river—
sometimes calm,
sometimes restless,
sometimes deeply silent.

Hidden inside the green and red bars were human fear, hope, and memory.
That was when I first felt—
"A chart is not merely lines; it is the history of human emotion."
Behind every candle stands a person—
someone who buys,
someone who sells,
someone who waits.

A chart is the collective image of all those moments—
where millions of decisions merge into a single picture.

*This image is used from internet sources for reference only.

Every movement in the market tells a story.
When prices rise, someone somewhere is holding onto belief.
When prices fall, someone somewhere is afraid.

That is why I always say—
"Charts do not explain the market; they explain people."
If a trader only sees charts but fails to understand character,
he becomes a slave to numbers.

But the one who understands the reason behind the numbers
becomes a true student of the market.

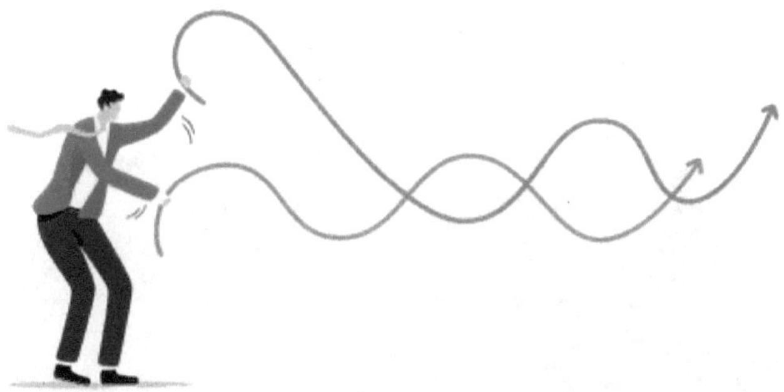

Once, I was teaching a young student how to read charts.
He was carefully counting candles one after another.
I asked him,
"What exactly are you seeing?"
He replied,
"Sir, prices are rising... red and green candles are forming patterns."
I smiled and said,
"And I see people in the market—
some crying, some smiling, some trapped in confusion."
He looked surprised and asked,
"What do you mean?"
I answered softly,
"You are seeing prices; I am seeing people."
That is the real difference—
between looking at a chart
and understanding a chart.

Drawing lines on a chart is easy.
But discovering the meaning behind those lines is difficult.
Because every line in the market is actually the mark of an emotion.

Some people call it "support,"
others call it "resistance."
I call it—
"The boundary line of human belief."

Charts never lie,
but we often look at them with false hopes.
And that hope becomes the beginning of mistakes.
The day we begin to see charts as mirrors of human behavior,
that is the day we truly learn—
seeing the market is not enough;
understanding it is what matters.

Summary

- Charts are maps of human emotions.
- Every candle represents a decision and a story.
- It is belief—not price—that drives the market.
- A trader's job is not only to see charts, but to understand them.

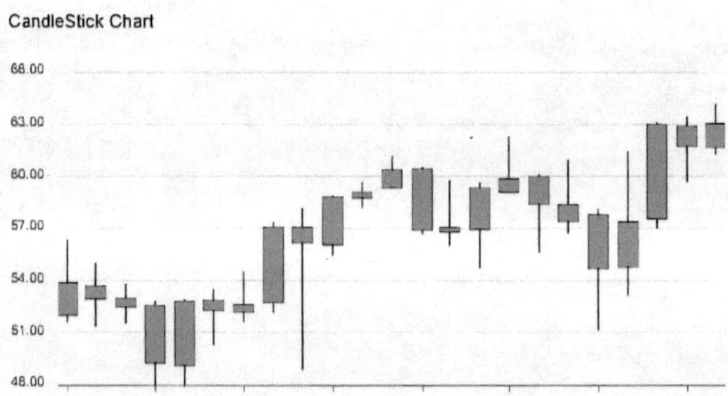

"A chart is not human, yet it speaks exactly like one—
if you know how to listen."

— BHOLANATH DAS

CHAPTER 5

Learn to Understand Trends, Not Indicators

*This image is used from internet sources for reference only.

One day, a student asked me,
"Sir, which indicator is the best?"
I replied,
"The best indicator is the one that keeps your mind calm."
Because in the market, every indicator is true—
and every indicator is false.
It becomes true when you know when to use it.
It becomes false when you do not know what to trust.
The greatest indicator in the market is the flow of time itself.

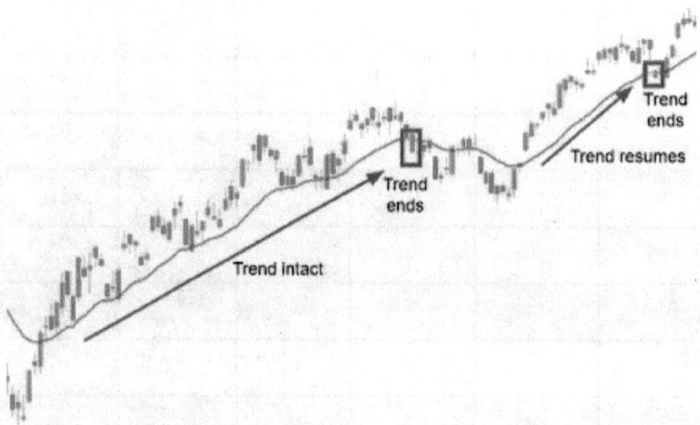

Everything has its own rhythm—
there are moments when prices rise excessively,
moments when the market pauses,
and moments when movement begins again.
These fluctuations are just like human breathing.
If a trader cannot understand this rhythm,
he gets lost inside numbers.
But the one who understands the rhythm of the market
aligns it with the rhythm of his own mind.

I always say—
"Indicators may give signals,
but decisions are made by your mind."
So if you truly want success in the market,
learn not only charts, but the character of time itself.
When the market is calm, rest.
When the market is unstable, become cautious.
That is what understanding trend truly means.

A market trend is like the current of a river.
If you swim against the current,
you may move a little,
but you will become exhausted very quickly.
But if you move with the current,
you can travel much farther with less effort.
The same is true in trading—
understanding and moving with the market trend
is the first lesson of a successful trader.

Summary

- Indicators only provide direction; your mind makes the decision.
- Understanding trend means understanding the rhythm of time
- Fighting against the trend wastes energy
- Success comes when you become one with the rhythm of the market.

"Not indicators—time itself is the greatest teacher."

— BHOLANATH DAS

CHAPTER 6

Timeframe — The Mirror of Time

*This image is used from internet sources for reference only.

One morning, I opened the Nifty chart and saw prices rising.
An hour later, prices were falling.
By afternoon, prices started rising again.
I thought to myself,
"What does this market actually want?"
Then I realized—
the market itself never changes;
only the mirror of time changes.

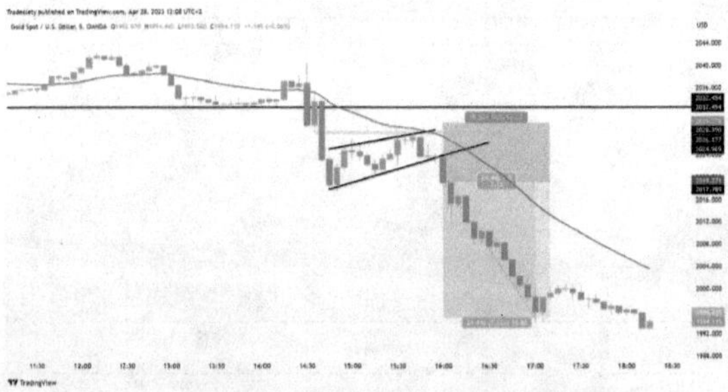

What appears to be a violent storm in a small timeframe
may look like a gentle breeze in a larger timeframe.
Just as a painful day in life,
after ten years, becomes a lesson.
Trading works the same way—

On a 5-minute chart, there is fear.
On a 1-hour chart, there is hope.
On a daily chart, there is reality.
On a monthly chart, there is philosophy.
The trader who sees only one timeframe
becomes one-sided in thinking.
But the trader who combines all timeframes together
becomes an observer, a thinker, and eventually a winner.

I often tell my students—
"Change the timeframe, and your perspective will change."
The market may be the same,
the price may be the same,
yet the interpretation becomes completely different.
That is the wonder of the market—
the way you look at it determines what it shows you.

Time is the only true mirror
where you can see your own patience.
The trader who understands monthly charts with patience
knows that losses may come, but he will not break emotionally.
But the one who watches only minute charts
may earn profits, yet lose peace of mind.

"The market does not change with time;
time changes our perspective."

— BHOLANATH DAS

Summary

- The meaning of the market changes with time.
- Small timeframes create fear; larger timeframes create understanding.
- Changing the timeframe means changing perspective.
- Patience is the greatest weapon of a trader.

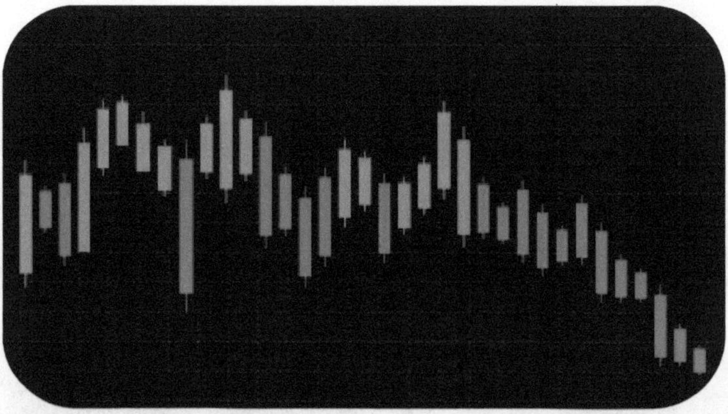

"The market does not change with time; time changes our perspective."

— BHOLANATH DAS

CONCLUSION

"Beyond charts lies character,
beyond indicators lies experience,
and beyond time lies patience—
these three qualities create a true trader."

*This image is used from internet sources for reference only.

PART 3

The Design of the System

A story of rules, discipline, and creating one's own path.

CHAPTER 7

From Thought to System

Many people in the market say—
"Trading without a system is like sailing in the ocean without direction."

When I first started trading,
I also had no direction.

I used to sell out of fear,
buy after hearing news,
and finally become frustrated thinking—
"The market is unfair."

One day, a senior trader told me,
"The market is not unfair; you are simply unprepared."
That day became a turning point in my life.

I sat down and began writing my own rules—

- When I would trade
- When I would stop
- How much loss I would tolerate
- And most importantly—when I would do nothing at all

That "doing nothing" became the strongest rule in my system.

A trader's greatest enemy is not the market—
it is his own restlessness.
And to control that restlessness, rules are necessary. A system does not simply mean code or software. A system means disciplined thinking. The moment you know why you are entering a trade and when you should stop, that is the moment you truly enter a system.

I have seen many students— they change indicators, they change timeframes, but they never change their habits. So I tell them—

"The market will change, but unless you change yourself, nothing will truly change."

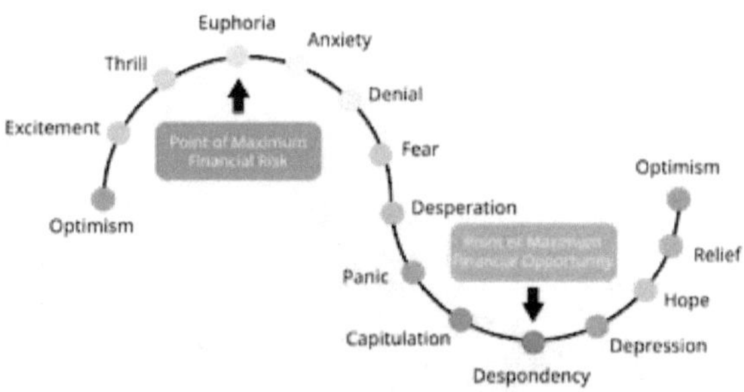

The Cycle of Market Emotions

A good trading system never guarantees profit. Instead, it teaches you how to survive losses. Because in the market, survival itself is the first success. Many traders know how to enter a trade, but very few know how to exit.

Some enter with confidence, but exit with fear. A true system teaches both entry and exit with clarity. And above all, it teaches emotional control.

I realized one important truth—
"A trader without discipline eventually becomes a victim of his own emotions."

Summary

- A system is not software; it is disciplined thinking.
- Rules reduce emotional mistakes.
- Survival in the market is more important than quick profit.
- A trader must learn not only entry, but also exit.

*"To defeat the market is not the goal;
you need a system to control your own restlessness."*

— BHOLANATH DAS

CHAPTER 8

Discipline — The Invisible Strength

In the market, everyone searches for strategy, but very few search for discipline. Yet in reality, strategy may show the path, but discipline helps a person walk on it. I once saw a trader who knew many indicators, many setups, and many market theories.

But every time he suffered a small loss, he broke his own rules. One day I asked him, "If you do not trust your own rules, then why create them at all?" He remained silent. That silence itself carried the answer.

Discipline is not about controlling the market. It is about controlling yourself. The market will rise and fall. News will change every day. People around you will panic, become greedy, or emotional. But the trader who remains steady within himself slowly becomes stronger than the market's noise.

I have realized one thing— most losses do not come from lack of knowledge, but from lack of self-control. That is why discipline is invisible, yet it is the strongest power in trading.

A disciplined trader knows when not to trade. He understands that every opportunity is not meant for him. Many traders lose money not because the market is wrong, but because they force themselves into unnecessary trades.

The market is like the ocean— sometimes calm, sometimes dangerous. A wise sailor does not sail during every storm. Likewise, a wise trader also waits for the right moment.

I often tell my students— "Patience is also a position." When you avoid a bad trade, you are still making a good decision. This understanding changes everything. Because trading is not only about action.

Sometimes the greatest skill is restraint. The market rewards not the fastest trader, but the most balanced one.

Summary

- Discipline is stronger than strategy.
- Most losses come from emotional decisions, not lack of knowledge.
- A good trader knows when to stay away from the market.
- Patience and restraint are powerful trading skills.

*"A machine can give signals,
but only a calm mind can make decisions."*

— BHOLANATH DAS

CHAPTER 9

Loss — The Greatest Teacher

No trader can avoid loss. Loss is not a sign of failure; it is part of the journey. But most people fear loss so much that they stop learning from it. When I faced my early losses, I used to blame the market, the news, even luck. But gradually I understood— the market was not punishing me. It was teaching me.

Every loss carries a message. Some losses teach patience. Some teach risk management. Some teach humility. And sometimes, a single mistake teaches more than a hundred profitable trades. A trader who accepts loss calmly becomes emotionally stronger. But the trader who refuses to accept mistakes keeps repeating them again and again.

I remember one trade very clearly. I ignored my own rules because I felt "confident." At first, the trade moved slightly in my favor. Then suddenly the market reversed. Instead of accepting the loss, I kept hoping. That hope slowly turned into a disaster.

That day I learned— "Hope is dangerous when it replaces discipline."
Since then, I stopped treating losses as enemies. I began treating them as lessons.

I once told a student,
"If you see everything moving upward while you are moving downward, then the problem is not with the market, but with your direction."

Understanding the market's "direction" means understanding the flow of time. Where there is fear in the flow, remain calm.

Where there is hope in the flow, participate.

Summary

- Biasness means understanding the psychological direction of the market.
- A trader's job is not to follow small waves, but to move with the larger trend.
- Understanding the emotional flow of time brings stability in decision-making.

*"If the market direction is right,
even small mistakes do not lead to losses."*

— BHOLANATH DAS

Conclusion

"To survive in the market,
strategy is not the real weapon —a system of thinking is."

*This image is used from internet sources for reference only.

PART 4

Option Trading — The Real World

The Story of Probability, Risk, and Self-Discipline

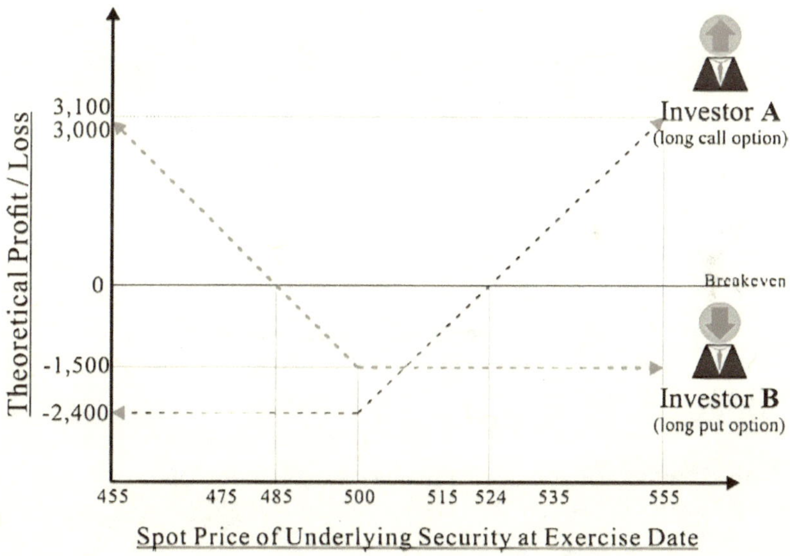

CHAPTER 10

The Illusion of Easy Profit

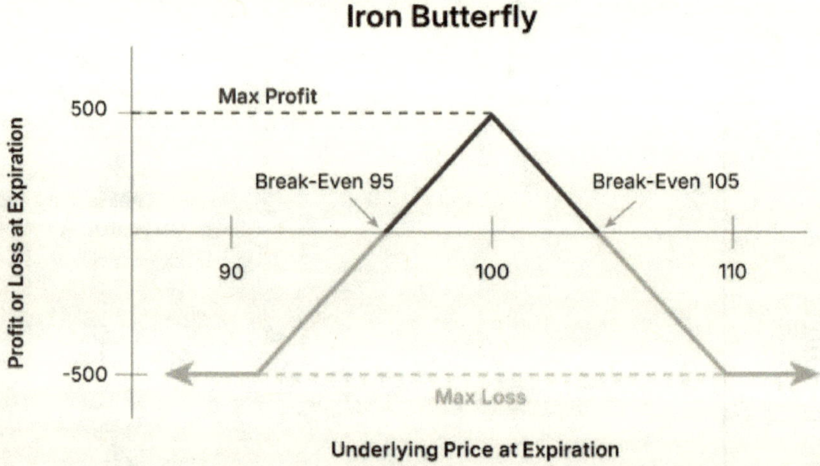

I still remember that afternoon.
Sourav entered my office — a young student, fearful in his eyes, worried on his face.
He said,
"Sir, I bought a call option, but the market isn't moving.
My premium is decreasing!"

I looked at him silently and said,
"Do you know what you actually bought?"
He thought for a moment and said, "Sir, I bought a chance to make a profit."

I laughed and said,
"No Sourav, you bought time decay.
If the market doesn't move, that time decay will decrease every day."

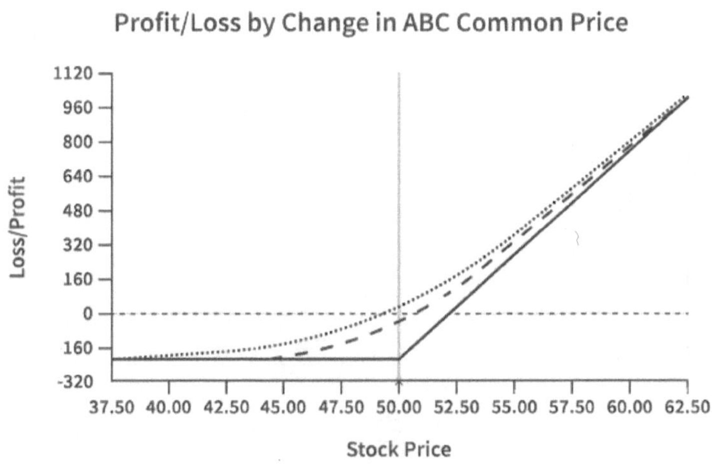

Real Example

Nifty was at 22,000 then.
Sourav bought a 22,200 call option at ₹100.
Three days later, Nifty was still 22,020.
But his premium dropped to ₹60.

He was surprised, "The market hasn't gone down, so why the loss?"
I said,
"Because when the market doesn't move, time moves.
And battling time is impossible."

Lesson
Option trading means earning profit quickly,
rather, it's about understanding the right timing with patience.

"Teaching options trading,
the true premium is the value of time."

— BHOLANATH DAS

Chapter 11

Premium, Greeks and Reality

One day, another one of my students, Rohit, came carrying a pile of notebooks.
He was struggling with the Greeks — Delta, Gamma, Theta, Vega...
I could see fear in his eyes.

He said, "Sir, I don't understand anything, but everyone says you can't trade without knowing the Greeks."

I smiled and asked,
"When you drive a car, do you understand every screw inside the engine?"

He replied, "No, Sir."

"Yet the car still runs! In the same way, Greeks are not just formulas — they are the story of time, speed, and expectations."

The Sweet Shop Example

I told him,
"A hot rasgulla has just been made — its price is ₹20.
In the evening, when it becomes cold, the shopkeeper will sell it for ₹15. Why?"

Rohit said,
"Because as time passes, the taste becomes less enjoyable."

I replied,
"In the same way, the hotter the market expectations are, the higher the premium becomes.
And when expectations cool down, the premium falls."

*This image is used from internet sources for reference only.

Greeks Made Simple

Greek	Meaning	Comparison
Delta	Impact when prices move	Floating on the waves
Theta	Waste of time	The sand of the hourglass
Vega	Uncertainty	Weather
Gamma	Change of speed	Speed of the wave

Fear vanished from Rohit's eyes.
He said, "Then even if I memorize the formula, can I try to understand it?"
I said,
"Yes, it lives not in the trader's formula, but in the feeling."

Lesson
Understanding the Greeks means understanding the market's mood.
You can be mathematical, but if you are not calm, you will lose.

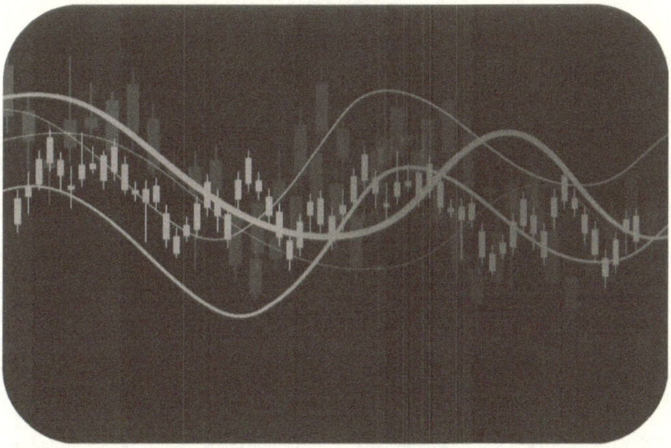

"The Greeks do not teach how to win,
they teach where to stay peaceful."

— BHOLANATH DAS

CHAPTER 12

The story of spread, hedge, and failure

It was 10 p.m. Then.
My student Joy said on the phone in a panicked voice,
"Sir, I have lost everything. The market has turned upside down."

I asked,
"Did you hedge?"
He said, "No, sir. I thought this time there would be no mistake."

I said quietly,
"The market forgives mistakes, but not arrogance."

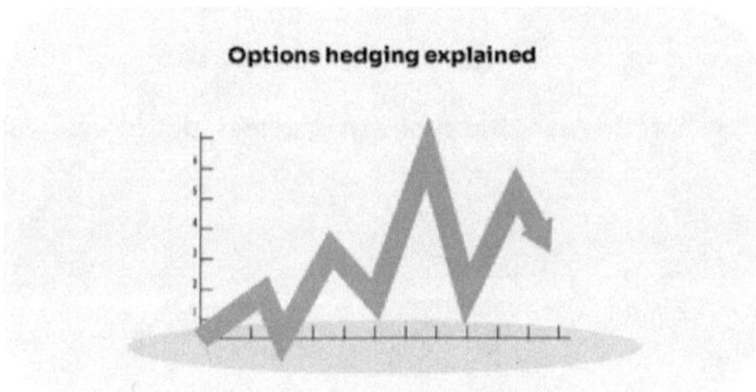

What is Hedging?

I asked Joy,
"You don't put the tarp on the house before the rain?"
He said, "I do."
"Then why don't you put a roof in the market too?"

Hedge means roof —
You cannot prevent loss, but you can reduce it.

Real example — Bull Call Spread

Nifty at 22,000.
Bought a 22,200 Call at a premium of ₹100.
At the same time, sold a 22,400 Call at a premium of ₹50.
Total cost: ₹50.

If the price exceeds 22,400, the profit is ₹150.
If the price does not increase, the maximum loss is ₹50.

I said,
"This is a bull call spread — limited profit, limited loss, but a peaceful sleep."

Illustration

```
Profit ↑
 |         -------
 |       /
 | ----------/------------- Price →
     ↑
Break-even
```

Joy smiled and said,
"Sir, it feels like I've learned not to fear the market, but to understand it."

I replied,
"The fear of the market fades when you know how far your loss can go."

Lesson
Hedging means wisdom, and spreads mean balance.
A successful trader is not a player of profits, but a player of survival.

"Option trading does not teach you to win, it teaches you to survive."

— BHOLANATH DAS

CHAPTER 13

Covered call — income from shares

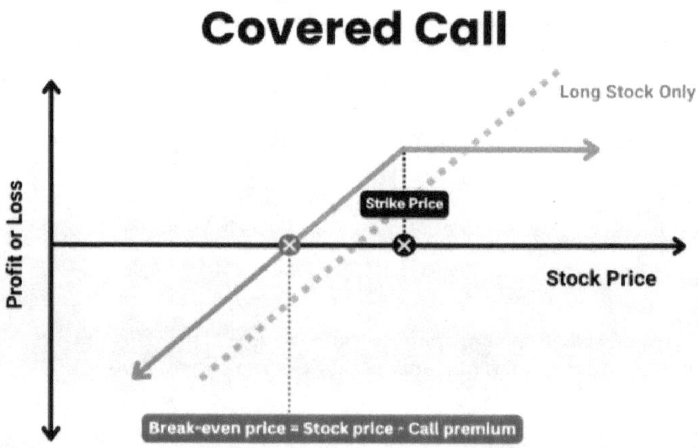

*This image is used from internet sources for reference only.

A trader I knew, Ramesh, always used to say,
"Sir, I only hold shares. I never sell anything."

I replied,
"Then your shares are just sitting at home doing nothing.
Put them to work — in the options market."

He was surprised.
I said,
"You hold 100 shares of Tata Consultancy Services at ₹4,000.
Now sell a 4,200 Call at a premium of ₹80.

If the price does not rise, you will earn ₹8,000.
And even if the price rises, you will sell the shares at a profit."
Ramesh was amazed, "You mean I can earn while still holding the shares!"

I said,
"This is called a covered call — professional income for a calm investor."

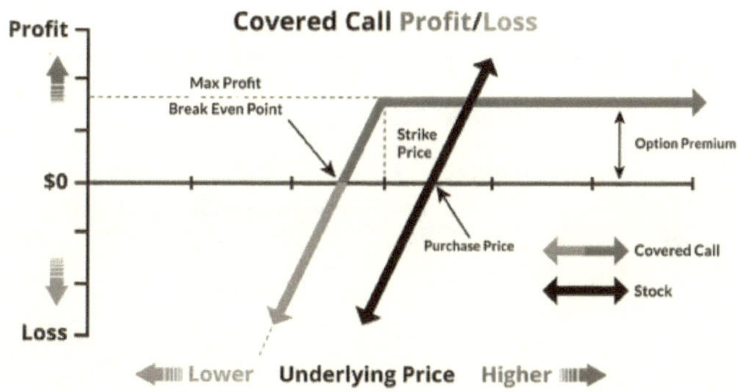

CHAPTER 14

Protective Put — The Philosophy of Insurance

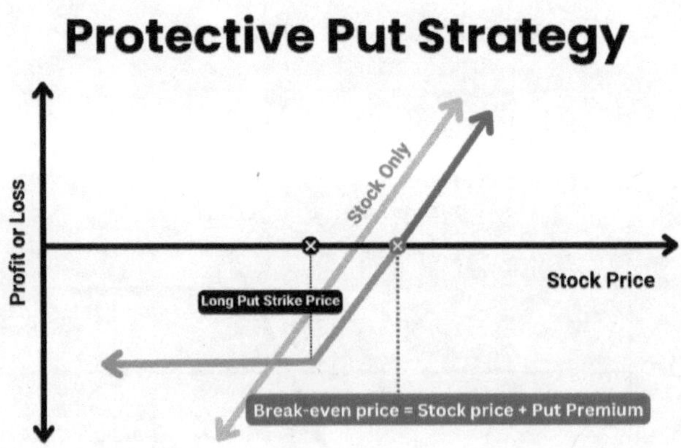

*This image is used from internet sources for reference only.

A student named Tanmay was afraid whenever prices fell.
I told him,
"Just as you keep insurance in life, you should keep insurance in the market too."

He was holding 100 shares of Infosys at ₹1500.
I told him,
"Buy a 1480 Put for ₹20."

The price fell to 1460.
He made a profit of ₹20 on the Put, and the loss on his shares was covered.

Tanmay smiled and said,
"Sir, now I feel at peace."

I replied,
"In the market, peace cannot be bought,
but with hedging, it is created."

CHAPTER 15

Iron Condor — Profiting in a Quiet Market

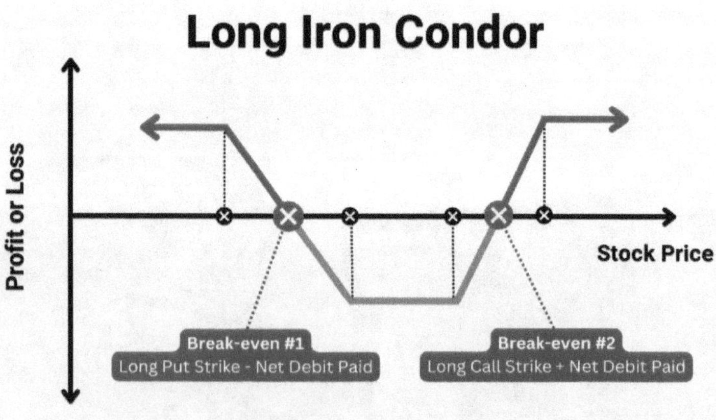

*This image is used from internet sources for reference only.

CHAPTER 15

Iron Condor — Profiting in a Quiet Market

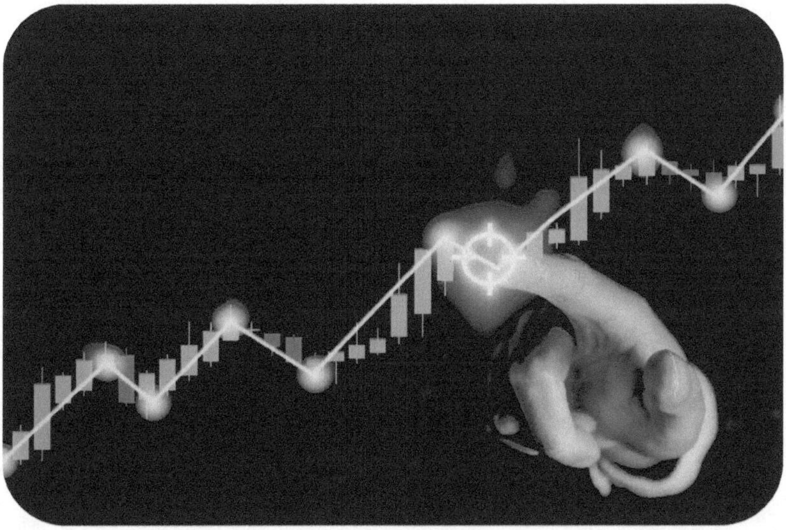

*This image is used from internet sources for reference only.

A student asked, "Sir, the market is completely stable. How can we trade in this situation?"
I replied,
"When the river is calm, let the boat float in the middle."
I drew on the board —

```
Profit ↑

|
| ________________
| /
|
| ________________/________________ Price →
|
↑
Break-Even
```

Nifty at 22,000.
Sell the 21,000 Put, sell the 23,000 Call,
and buy two farther strikes for safety.
If the market stays within the middle range, you keep the premium from both sides.

I said,
"This is an Iron Condor —
even when the market does not move, income is possible."

CHAPTER 16

Calendar Spread — Earning from Time

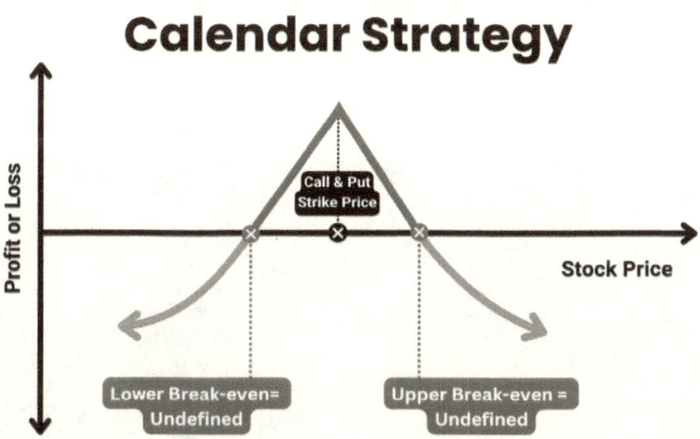

*This image is used from internet sources for reference only.

In the options market, time is money.
One day, I said,
"You sell a one-month option and hold a long-term option."

The student was surprised.
"Sir, what is the profit in that?"

I replied,
"Short-term options melt away quickly,
while long-term options melt slowly.
This difference is your income."

A Nifty 22,000 Call was priced at ₹140 in August and ₹100 in July.
If you sell the July option and buy the August option,
as time passes, the July option will fall to zero,
and you will earn a profit of ₹40.

*This image is used from internet sources for reference only.

CHAPTER 17

Emotional Hedge — The Art of Controlling the Mind

*This image is used from internet sources for reference only.

In options trading, the greatest hedge is a calm mind.

Sometimes the market suddenly creates fear.
I say,
"Keep a small opposite position — it is your mental helmet."

For example, if you are in a buy position,
holding a small put option will remind you —
"I am not completely unprotected."

This confidence keeps the mind steady.
Traders who maintain a mental hedge in the market
survive not through panic, but through analysis.

*This image is used from internet sources for reference only.

CONCLUSION

Options trading is a delicate balance between time, fear, and probability.
Here, you may earn profits in a single day, suffer losses in a week, and gain wisdom over a lifetime.

*This image is used from internet sources for reference only.

"An options trader knows — opportunities do not come all the time, but if you stay prepared, once is enough."

— BHOLANATH DAS

Summary:

Strategy	Goal	Risk	Lesson
Covered call	Income from shares	Limited	Stability
Protective put	Share security	Limited	Self-confidence
Bull Call Spread	Slight increase	Defined	Patience
Iron Condor	Profit in a stable market	Limited	Peace
Calendar spread	Income from time	Limited	Plan
Emotional hedge	Mental control	Minimum	Peace

mirror_mod.use_z = False
elif _operation == "MIRROR_Y":
mirror_mod.use_x = False
mirror_mod.use_y = True
mirror_mod.use_z = False
elif _operation == "MIRROR_Z":
mirror_mod.use_x = False
mirror_mod.use_y = False
mirror_mod.use_z = True

1138,24
1267,21 0,08

PART 5

Path and Realization

Life Lessons from the Market

CHAPTER 13

Mind and Map

*This image is used from internet sources for reference only.

CHAPTER 13

Mind and Map

Every morning when I sit down to open the chart,
the colors on the screen change, prices go up and down.
But inside, another price goes up and down —
that of my mind.

One day I realized, to win in the market
it is not understanding the chart that matters, but understanding your own map.

Inside each of us, there is a map —
filled with the paths of fear, greed, hope, patience, and memory.
This very map decides,
where we stop, where we leap, where we retreat.

*This image is used from internet sources for reference only.

I once told a student,
"I don't care how much you trade, if you don't know yourself, you won't be able to survive in the market for long."

The market tests the mind —
The day you rush, it teaches you patience.
The day you act with pride, it teaches you humility.
The day you run away in fear, it teaches you steadiness.

These lessons cannot be bought with money.
They come with time, through mistakes.

The map of the market is never complete,
just like the map of life.
But every day we draw new lines on it —
with the ink of experience.

*This image is used from internet sources for reference only.

Summary

- The real map of trading is inside.
- The market's mistakes are what teach patience and composure.
- Success means understanding your own mind, not the market.

"Beyond the charts, there is another map — that is the mind of a trader."

— BHOLANATH DAS

CHAPTER 14

Why Some People Become Successful

In the same market, some succeed, some fail.
Why?

Everyone looks at the same prices, the same charts, the same news.
That day I was thinking — where lies the difference?

The difference is not in strategy, but in **mindset.**

The person who is not afraid of mistakes, moves forward.
The person who accepts loss, learns.
The person who stays patient, wins.

Every day in the market, it is seen —
a small investor stands like a mountain after years,
while some others cannot survive even with big capital.

Because the first one has learned to fight with time,
the second one has learned to rush.

I always tell my students —
"No matter how much money you earn,
the greater lesson is not to lose your mind."
Because money can be lost and regained,
but if your mind breaks, it cannot be recovered.

Successful people know —
their greatest victory is not in the market,
but in conquering the fear within themselves.

Summary

- Success is not a technique, it is mental balance.
- Loss is an opportunity to learn, not defeat.
- Victory means controlling fear.

*This image is used from internet sources for reference only.

"In the market, profit is not the real wealth — mental stability is."

— BHOLANATH DAS

CHAPTER 15

The Path to Freedom

Years passed in the market.
Many profits, many losses, many experiences.
One day, I wondered —
"What am I really searching for?"

Money?
No, because after a point, even that becomes enough.
Then what?

I was searching for freedom.

The market is a strange place —
here, no one forces you.
You are your own teacher, student, and examiner.
The more control you have over yourself,
the freer you become.

"In the market, profit is not the real wealth — mental stability is."

— BHOLANATH DAS

A true trader never trades only for profit.
He trades to understand —
time, himself, and the world.

When you learn patience in the market, patience begins to appear in other parts of life as well.
When you become humble in the market, ego fades in life too.
In this way, the market transforms us from within.

In the end, I realized —
the market is not about income, but about insight.
The one who gains this understanding never truly loses.

Summary

- Trading is a path to self-discovery.
- Money is not the ultimate goal — freedom is.
- The market teaches life, if you are willing to learn.

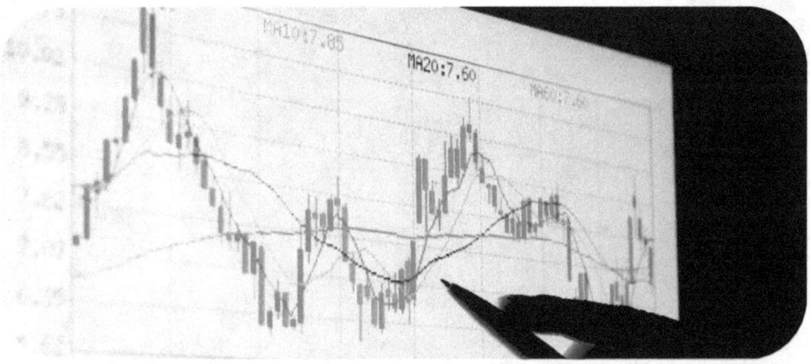

*This image is used from internet sources for reference only.

"Trading in the market does not mean winning every time, it means being at peace with yourself."

— BHOLANATH DAS

CONCLUSION

"In the end, I realized the market is not my mirror — it is my teacher."

*This image is used from internet sources for reference only.

"An options trader knows —
opportunities do not come all the time,
but if you stay prepared, even one opportunity is enough."

— BHOLANATH DAS

PART 6

The Silent Lessons

What books cannot teach, time does.

What books cannot teach, time does.

*This image is used from internet sources for reference only.

CHAPTER 16

The Illusion of Certainty

*This image is used from internet sources for reference only.

A single day of loss may make you cry,
but it gives you the wisdom of a thousand days.
In the market, loss means learning.
The day I suffered a big loss,
was the day I first searched for peace within myself.
I realized —
"Loss does not mean losing something,
rather, it means learning something extra."

The market teaches humility.
The day you think you know everything,
is the day it silences you.

Loss is that slap
which breaks arrogance and steadies the mind.

Summary

- Loss means education.
- The market does not tolerate arrogance.
- Peace comes from acceptance, not revenge.

"Accepting a loss is not defeat, it is maturity."

— BHOLANATH DAS

CHAPTER 17

SILENCE — A TRADER'S COMPANION

No matter how noisy the market becomes,
the successful trader becomes even quieter.

I always notice that new traders search for noise —
"Where is the signal?"
"Which news matters?"
"What did the influencer say?"

But experienced traders search for silence.
Because only a silent mind can hear the subtle rhythm of the market.

I have learned that the biggest decisions come after silence.
When the market pauses,
that is when opportunities are born.

A trader who can wait quietly
understands the language of the market.

*This image is used from internet sources for reference only.

Summary

- Silence is a trader's greatest strength.
- Opportunities come after patience.
- Staying quiet means staying steady.

"Not the noise of the market,
but silence gives the real signal."

— BHOLANATH DAS

PART 7

Final Words — The Story of Human Beings

One day, a student asked me,
"Sir, what have you learned after all these years?"
I smiled and said,
"The market is not about money; it is about building a friendship with time."

There was a time when I thought trading meant freedom.
Now I know trading means **responsibility.**
Responsibility for your own decisions, responsibility for your own mistakes, and responsibility for your own peace of mind.
It is this responsibility that matures a person.
The person who can accept his own mistakes —
he is the real trader, he is the real human being.

In the end, I realized —
the market is a vast classroom,
where every day brings a new lesson, a new test, and a new realization.
Some pass, while some return again and again.
But the one who learns with sincerity
never truly fails.

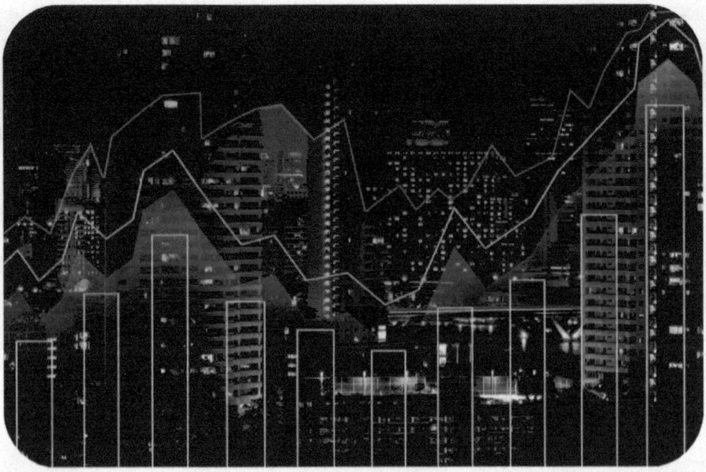

FINAL QUOTE

"What I learned from the market,
I applied not just on charts,
but in life."
— Bholanath Das

He searched for people within charts,
and searched for the market within people.

This book is the story of that experience —
the lessons the stock market teaches, but no one talks about.

*"The market is not my profession,
it is my philosophy."*

— BHOLANATH DAS

BALRO (Daily) 330.16
MA(50) 330.22
MA(200) 394.69
Volume 4,737, 850
MADD(12,26,9) -1.721, -3.475, 1.754

PART 8

The Symphony of Technology — A New Horizon of Skill

Where Technology and Mind Play in Perfect Harmony

*This image is used from internet sources for reference only.

INTRODUCTION

A person who understands only psychology in the market is only half a trader.
And a person who understands only charts is also half a trader.
But the one who can combine both —
is a complete trader.

In this chapter, we will learn that "skill"
which makes psychology and technology work together —
not through complicated formulas, but **through simple yet deep observation.**

"The market is not my profession,
it is my philosophy."

— BHOLANATH DAS

CHAPTER 18

The Melody of Price — Listening to the Flow

I once told a student,
"You don't just look at charts — you listen to their rhythm."
Surprised, he asked,
"Does the market have a sound too?"

I replied,
"When the price keeps returning to the same level again and again,
it feels as if the market is saying —
"This is where I feel comfortable.'"

That place is called the Mean Level —
where both price and psychology seek balance together.

*This image is used from internet sources for reference only.

Example

The Nifty keeps rising from 22,000 to 22,200 again and again, then falling back.
This is the market's "high musical note" –
when the price repeatedly touches the same note,
it shows that there is excessive excitement in the market.

```
Price ↑

|        /\   /\/\
|
|        /\  /\/\
|
|————————————————————————————————————→ Price
   ↑
 Mean Reversion Zone
```

Lesson

- Repetition in price reflects the market's emotional limit.
- Every price carries an emotion – fear, hope, or exhaustion.
- A true listener is the trader who understands not just the price, but the mind behind it.

CHAPTER 19

Momentum and Pause — The Rhythm of Momentum

The movement of the market is important, but its pauses are valuable too.
Those who fear pauses do not understand the market's "breathing."

Example

NIFTY BANK rose 2,000 points in three days.
On the fourth day, it paused, moving within just 100 points.
This pause is not weakness — it is rest,
a breath taken after a long run.

```
Price ↑

| ↑ ↑ ↑ ↑ ↑ ↑ ↑ ↑
|
| ↓ ↓
|
| ---- (Pause)
|
| ↑ ↑ ↑ ↑ ↑ ↑ ↑
|
•  └──────────────────────────────────→ Price
```

Lesson

- A pause does not mean weakness; it means preparation.
- Understanding momentum means learning to recognize pauses.

CHAPTER 20

The Shadow of Volume — The Hidden Language of the Crowd

*This image is used from internet sources for reference only.

Volume is the voice of the crowd.
When the price rises but volume does not increase, confidence is weak.
When the price remains stable but volume increases, strength is building internally.

Example

One day, Reliance Industries rose by 2%, but the volume was low.
On another day, the price moved only slightly, but the volume tripled — that was the day the real trend began.

Lesson

- Volume is the measure of conviction.
- Price speaks, volume provides the proof.

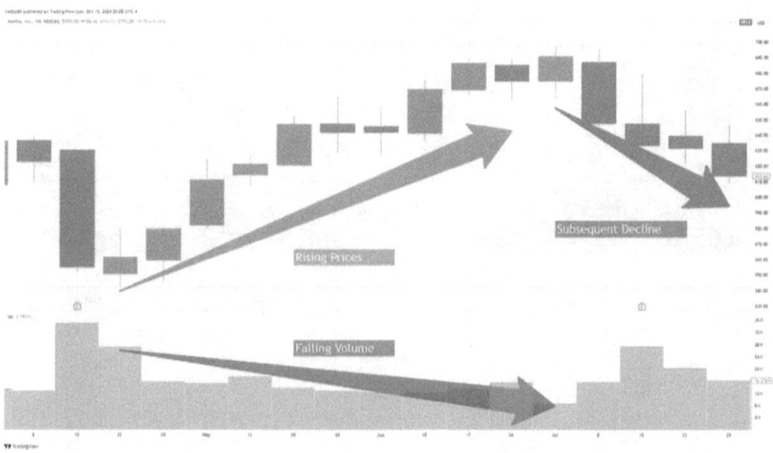

CHAPTER 21

Confluence of Time Frames — Harmony of Time

*This image is used from internet sources for reference only.

A student said, “Sir, I trade on the 5-minute chart, but I keep losing.”
I replied, “You are watching the waves of the river, but not the current.”

To understand the market, you must look at both small and large timeframes together.

"Small Chart:" ↑ ↓ ↑ ↓ ↑

"Big Chart:" ↗ ↗ ↗ ↗ ↗

Lesson:

- To understand the smaller timeframe, it is essential to know the direction of the larger timeframe.
- Alignment of timeframes means a calm and steady mind.

*This image is used from internet sources for reference only.

CHAPTER 22

Patterns of Probability — Human Behaviour

*This image is used from internet sources for reference only.

Patterns are the repetition of human thinking.
When people become optimistic, prices rise.
When they grow tired, prices stop moving.
When they become fearful, prices fall.

There are no "Head and Shoulders" in the market —
there are images of human confidence, fear, and exhaustion.

Lesson:

- Patterns are the shape of thought.
- What appears on the chart is the story of people.

*This image is used from internet sources for reference only.

CHAPTER 23

Technology and Humanity — The Bridge to the Future

*This image is used from internet sources for reference only.

Today, AI draws charts and robots place orders,
yet the final decision still belongs to humans.
Machines do not feel — humans do.
The trader who uses technology without losing emotion and intuition,
is the trader of the future.

Lesson:
Technology is a tool; the mind is the driver.
Human intuition complements technology.

*This image is used from internet sources for reference only.

CHAPTER 24

The Precise Rhythm of Technology — The Three Best Patterns

Introduction

Here, we will explore three high-accuracy patterns –

- Ascending Triangle
- Descending Triangle
- Pole & Flag

These are among the most practical and accurate patterns in the market, where consistency and stability play the key role.

Ascending Triangle – The Stairway of Patience

Each time, the price gets rejected at the same resistance level, but every low is higher than the previous one.

Ascending Triangle Pattern Formation

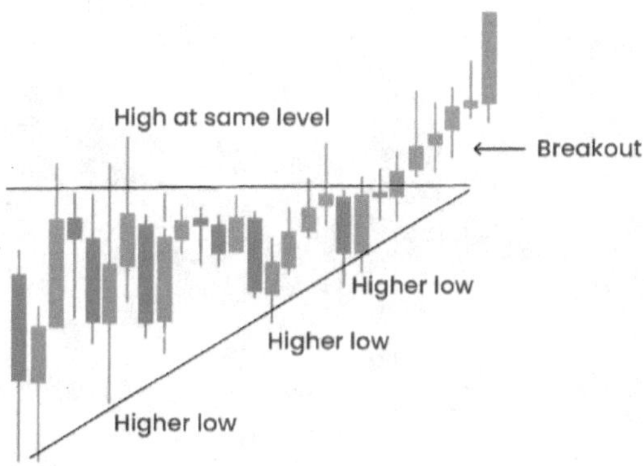

```
Price ↑
|
|     ———————————————————————— Resistance
|      /
|     /
|    /
| ______/_________________ Price →
```

It means the buyers are gradually increasing pressure.
Not just the price, confidence is rising too.

Lesson:

- In the market, patience is strength.
- Every higher low represents confidence.

*This image is used from internet sources for reference only.

Descending Triangle — The Pressure of Fear

Here, the price is holding the support every time,
but each high is lower than the previous one.

```
Price ↑
| \
|  \
|   \
|    \
| ____\__________ Support
|
└──────────────────────────── Price →
```

The sellers are taking control not out of panic, but out of habit.

Lesson:

- A Descending Triangle means calm control.
- Not panic, but restraint is the true maturity of the market.

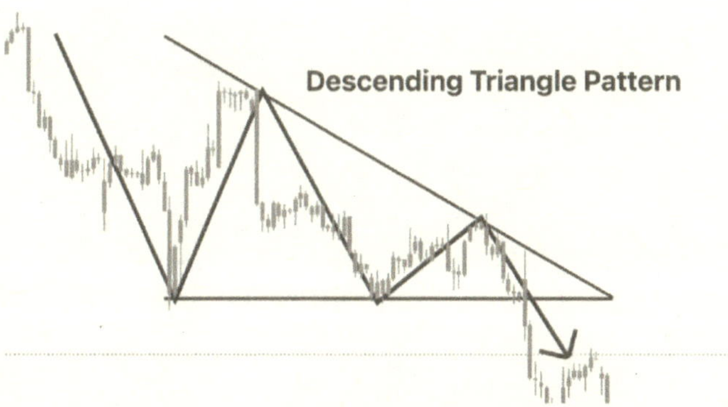

Pole & Flag – The Rhythm of Strength and Rest

After a strong momentum, the price moves in a small range.

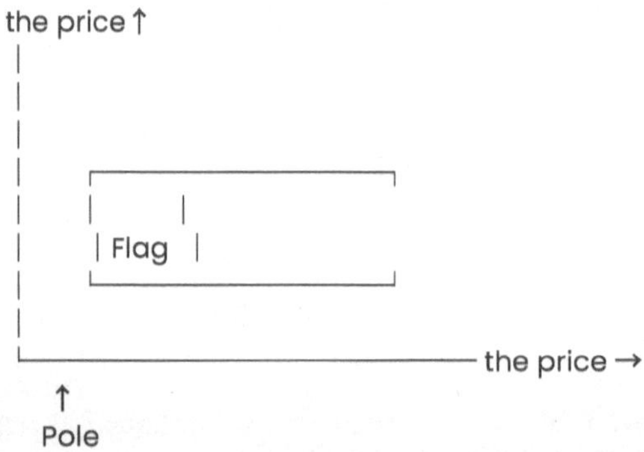

A flag means rest, not weakness.
The pole means momentum, and the flag means preparation.

Lesson:
When the market pauses, don't be afraid — stay alert.
The tighter the flag, the stronger the next move.

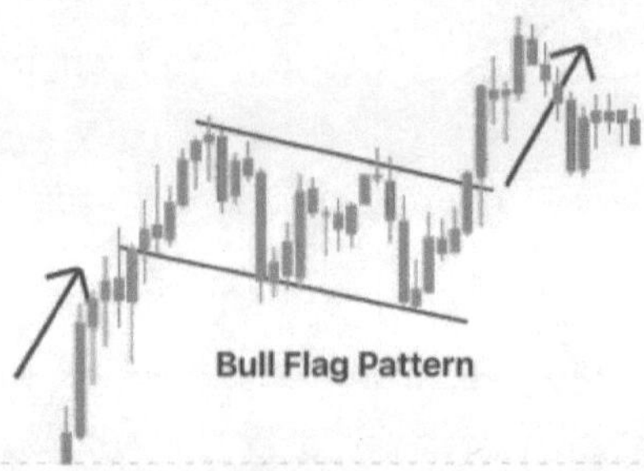

Comparative Philosophy

Pattern	Psychology	Message
Ascending Triangle	Buyer's patience	"I am prepared."
Descending Triangle	Seller's restraint	"I am steady."
Pole & Flag	Strength and rest	"I will return again."

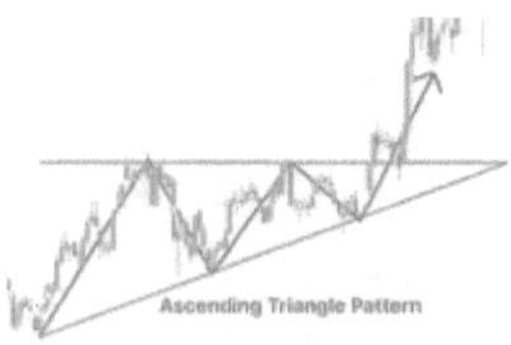

These three patterns teach us that—
a chart is not just lines, but the rhythm of human thinking.
Every movement in the market tells a story of human hope, fear, and patience.

"Success in market technology comes
when one can see the human within the lines."

— BHOLANATH DAS

SUMMARY

Skill / Expertise	Meaning / Wealth	Mental Education
Rhythm of Price	Repeating Trends	Attention / Focus
Momentum Rhythm	Balance of Motion and Rest	Patience
Volume Shadow	The Faith of the Crowd	Observation
Timeframe Harmony	Connection with Time	Balance
Human Pattern	Reflection of Behavior	Intuition
Tech & Human Blend	Technology and the Mind	Self-awareness
Ascending Triangle	The Rhythm of Patience	Stability
Descending Triangle	The Rhythm of Discipline	Outcome
Pole & Flag	The Rest of Strength	Preparation

"Understanding market patterns is not about reading charts, it is about reading the rhythm of people."

— BHOLANATH DAS

FINAL WORDS OF THE BOOK

This book is not a trading course.
It is the inner journey of a man — who evolved from a teacher to a researcher, from a researcher to a trader, and finally into a thoughtful observer.

PART 9

"The Truth Behind the Index"

What is an Index? (The Real Truth)

A new trader opens the chart in the morning and sees that the Nifty is green. He thinks, "The market is good today, so let me buy." But by afternoon, he ends up in a loss. Why? Because he only looked at the Index, but did not understand the market environment.

An Index is only the result, but the environment is the cause. If you make decisions by looking only at the result, then you are already late. Understanding why the market is rising or falling is far more important.

Imagine you are looking at an exam result. The result says you failed, but what is the reason? You did not study. In the same way, when you look at the Index, you only see the result, not the reason behind it.

Rule:
"Don't just look at the Index — understand why the Index became like this."

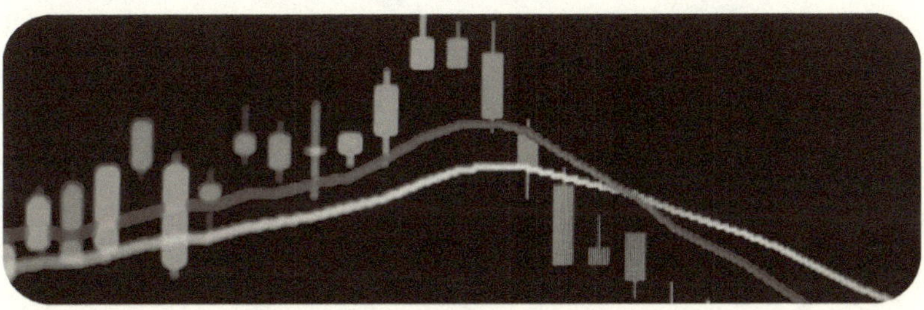

CHAPTER 2

Weightage (Impact of Weight)

Not all stocks are equal. Some large companies like Reliance Industries, HDFC Bank, and ICICI Bank carry more weight in the Index. That's why they have a greater impact on it.

Suppose Reliance rises by +4%, while 10 smaller stocks fall by -2%. In that case, the Index may still appear green, but in reality, the market is weak. In other words, the Index does not always tell the complete truth.

This creates a kind of distortion. Even if no one intentionally manipulates the market, the structure itself can create a misleading impression.

Rule:
"The Index is not the complete truth — it is a weighted truth."

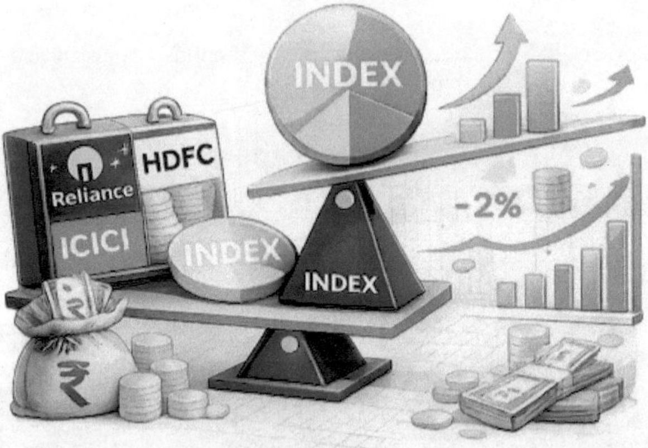

*Images in this book are used from internet sources for reference only.

CHAPTER 3

Index vs Market

An Index means an average, while the Market means participation. An index only shows the average, but it does not show how many stocks are actually participating.

Suppose, out of 50 stocks, 5 are performing very well while 45 are performing poorly. In that case, the Index may still look fine, but the market is actually weak.

It is like a classroom—just because 5 students are toppers does not mean the whole class is doing well. So, to understand the market, it is important to understand participation.

Rule:
"To understand the market, understand participation."

CHAPTER 4

Index Movement

The first stage is the Hidden Phase – here, smart money enters the market slowly, but the price does not move much.

The second stage is the Visible Phase — the price starts rising, and everyone begins to enter.

The third stage is the Exhaustion Phase — at the final moment, everyone jumps in, the price rises rapidly, and then suddenly reverses.

If you understand these three stages, you will be able to understand where the market currently stands.

Rule:
"When everyone sees it, it is already too late."

*Images in this book are used from internet sources for reference only.

CHAPTER 5

Institutional Flow

Retail traders make decisions by looking at price. But big players (FIIs and institutions) follow the flow.

Price can often be misleading, but flow usually tells the truth. If big players are buying, the market gets support.

So, trading based only on price can lead to mistakes.

Rule:
"Don't follow the price, follow the flow."

*Images in this book are used from internet sources for reference only.

CHAPTER 6

Sector Rotation

The market never stays the same all the time. Today the IT sector is strong; tomorrow the Banking sector may be strong.

That means the market remains the same, but the focus changes. Smart money rotates between sectors.

So, opportunity lies not in the index, but in the sectors.

Rule:
"Opportunity lies in sectors, not in the index."

*Images in this book are used from internet sources for reference only.

CHAPTER 7

Index Alignment

If both Nifty and Bank Nifty move in the same direction, trading becomes safer.

But if the movement of one does not match the other, it is considered a weak signal.

When alignment is present, confidence increases.

Rule:
"Without alignment, there is no confidence."

*Images in this book are used from internet sources for reference only.

CHAPTER 8

Breadth

Breadth means how many stocks are participating in the movement. It shows the market's internal strength.

Suppose the index is up by +1%, but 70% of stocks are in the red. Then the market is actually weak.

If you do not observe breadth, you may get the wrong impression.

Rule:
"If you ignore breadth, losses are certain."

*Images in this book are used from internet sources for reference only.

Time Behaviour

Opening strong but closing weak → distribution.

Opening weak but closing strong → accumulation.

The movement at the end of the day (closing) is the most important.

Rule:
"Closing tells the truth."

*Images in this book are used from internet sources for reference only.

CHAPTER 10

Liquidity

Liquidity is the oxygen of the market. When liquidity is present, price movements become smooth.

A breakout with low volume is usually false.

So, without liquidity, a move is not trustworthy.

Rule:
"Without liquidity, a move is not reliable."

*Images in this book are used from internet sources for reference only.

The Art of Understanding

Chart Pattern — Behaviour

Chart Patterns — Behaviour
Many people see chart patterns only as shapes or designs—such as triangles, flags, breakouts, etc. But the real truth is that a pattern is not just a shape; it represents the behaviour or psychology inside the market. When you see a pattern, you are actually seeing the hidden battle between buyers and sellers behind the price.

Many new traders think that a pattern means future prediction. But in reality, a pattern never predicts the future. It only gives an indication that something is forming in the market. In other words, some kind of pressure is building up, which may become the reason for a future movement. So, patterns should be viewed as expectations, not predictions.

The market always moves based on demand and supply. When buyers become stronger, the price moves upward; and when sellers become stronger, the price moves downward. Patterns visually show these changes in strength. For example, an ascending triangle shows that buyers are gradually becoming stronger, while a descending triangle shows that sellers are taking control.

THE ART OF UNDERSTANDING

Chart Patterns — Behaviour

One important thing to understand is this: taking an entry just by looking at a pattern is one of the biggest mistakes. Many traders enter a trade as soon as they see a breakout, but they fail to understand whether it is real or fake. That happens because they only see the shape, not the behaviour. Professional traders first observe how the price is reacting — whether it is holding, showing rejection, and how the volume behaves.

Imagine the market is in a compression phase. From the outside, it may seem like nothing is happening, but internally, energy is building up. It is just like the calm atmosphere before a storm. During this time, patience is necessary. When the breakout finally happens, the decision should be based on the strength of that breakout.

Another powerful concept is the failed move. When a breakout fails and the price moves in the opposite direction, it often gives the strongest signal. This is because many traders get trapped there. That trap creates opportunities for smart money. That is why a failed breakout can sometimes be even more powerful than a normal breakout.

While using chart patterns, the most important thing is understanding the context, behaviour, and reaction. If you trade only by looking at patterns, consistency will never come. But if you can understand the psychology behind the pattern, the market's movement will become much clearer.

CHAPTER 1

Why Patterns Matter? (The Real Truth)

Many new traders think that a pattern simply means a breakout. But the real truth is completely different. A pattern does not actually predict the future; rather, it reveals the internal pressure of the market. When a pattern forms, it means something is building underneath.

A pattern is not just a shape — it is an expectation. It means the market is not doing anything yet, but it is preparing for something to happen. This is the most important area, because this is where smart money operates.

Imagine slowly blowing air into a balloon. From the outside, nothing seems to be happening, but pressure is building inside. Eventually, it will burst. In the same way, a pattern shows the hidden energy building within the market.

Rule:
"A pattern is not a shape; a pattern is an expectation."

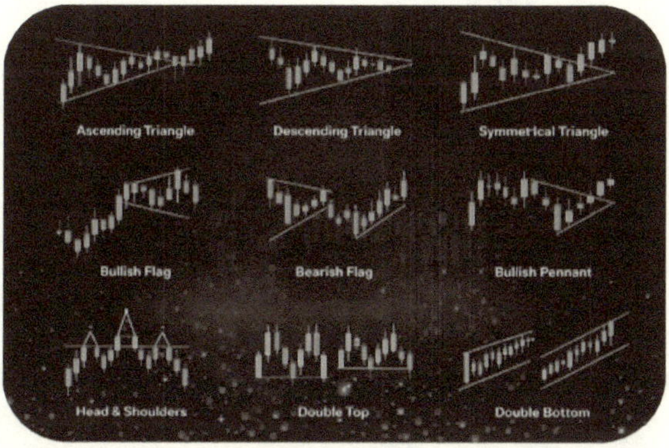

*Images in this book are used from internet sources for reference only.

CHAPTER 2

Ascending Triangle — The Patience of Buyers

In this pattern, the resistance stays at the same level, but the price lows gradually move higher. This means buyers are entering earlier and becoming more confident.

The seller keeps selling at the same level repeatedly, but the buyers are becoming increasingly aggressive. This shows that demand is rising.

Many people make the mistake of entering as soon as they see a breakout. But the real question is — is the price holding? Is there a fake rejection or not?

Imagine a student who keeps failing repeatedly, but improves their marks each time. Eventually, that student will pass.

Rule:
"Enter when you see a strong hold, not just because of a breakout."

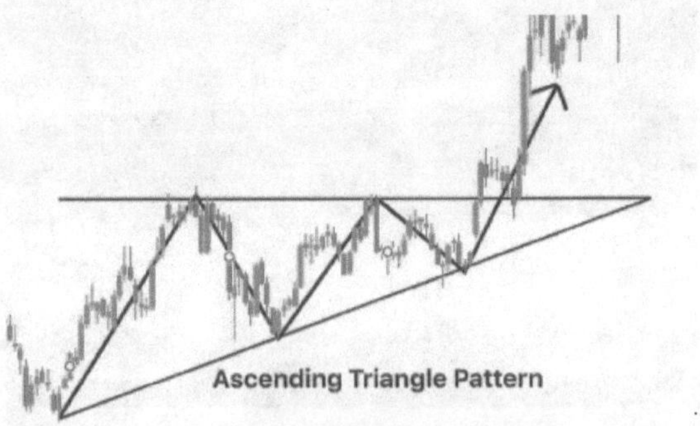

*Images in this book are used from internet sources for reference only.

CHAPTER 3

Descending Triangle — Controlled Selling

Here, the support level remains the same, but the highs gradually move downward. This shows that sellers are exiting the market in an organized manner.

This is not panic selling; rather, it is a planned exit. Sellers are slowly creating pressure.

Imagine a shopkeeper gradually reducing his inventory. It indicates that demand is decreasing.

Taking an entry immediately after the break is a mistake. After the break, the behavior of the market must be observed.

Rule:
"Not the break, but the behavior after the break is what matters."

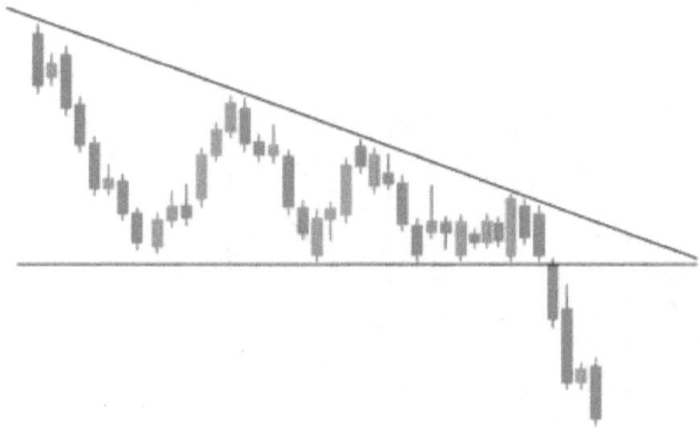

*Images in this book are used from internet sources for reference only.

CHAPTER 4

Pole & Flag — Momentum Digestion

In this pattern, there is first a strong move (the pole), followed by a small pause (the flag). This shows that the market is not tired — it is simply taking a pause.

Many traders enter as soon as they see the flag, but that can be risky. First, you should check whether the volume has decreased and whether the range is tight.

Imagine you are running and stop for a moment — it does not mean you are exhausted; it means you are preparing to run again.

After this pause, there is a possibility of another strong move.

Rule:
"Tight flag + hold = continuation."

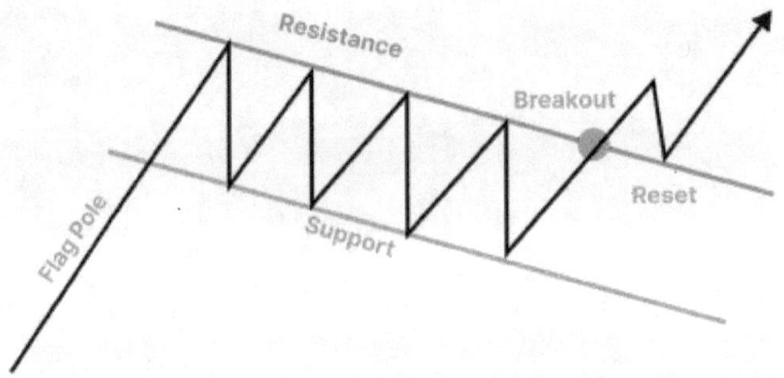

*Images in this book are used from internet sources for reference only.

Compression — Energy Build-up

In compression, the price range becomes smaller and the candles become smaller. This shows that energy is building up in the market.

During this time, the market stays calm, but pressure is building internally. It is like the silence before a storm.

Many people make the mistake of trying to predict the breakout direction. But more important than direction is strength.

A trade should only be taken if a strong movement appears after the breakout.

Rule:
"Don't focus on direction; focus on the strength after the breakout."

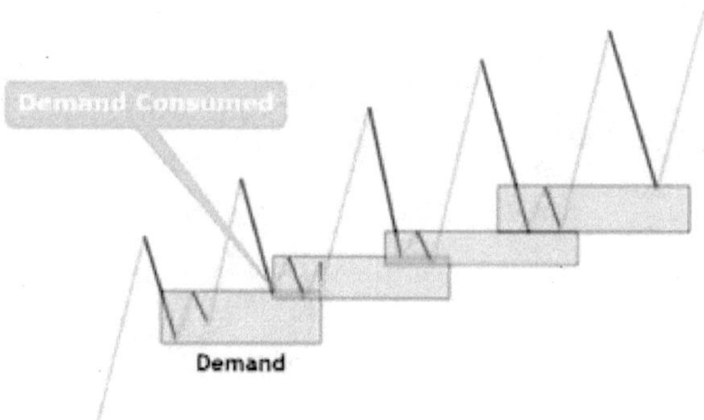

*Images in this book are used from internet sources for reference only.

CHAPTER 6

(Failed Move — The Most Powerful Pattern)

In this pattern, a breakout happens first, then it fails and reverses. This is one of the most powerful signals.

A trap is created here. Those who enter on the breakout get stuck.

Imagine someone starts running and suddenly falls — instead of moving forward, they turn back.

This failure itself creates the biggest opportunity.

Rule:
"Failed breakout = opposite trade."

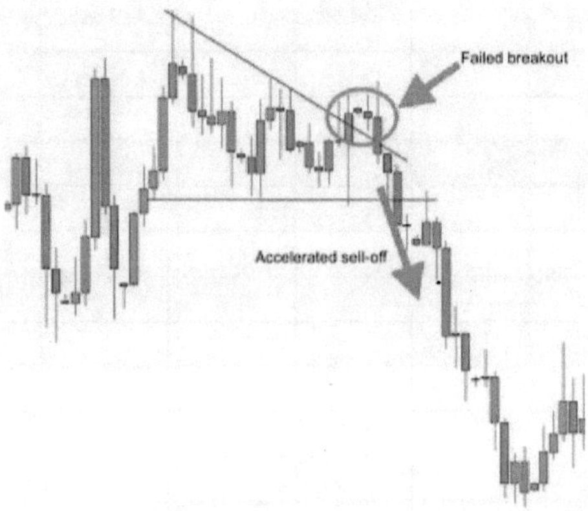

*Images in this book are used from internet sources for reference only.

09:25
09:30

09:30

PART 10

Beyond Patterns: The Real Science of Decision Making

Most people take entries just by looking at patterns.

They ignore context, volume, and behavior.

But professional traders think differently.

First, they identify the pattern, then they check the context.

After that, they observe the behavior, and finally take the entry.

Following this process brings consistency.

Final Wisdom:
"Patterns do not predict the future — they create expectations."

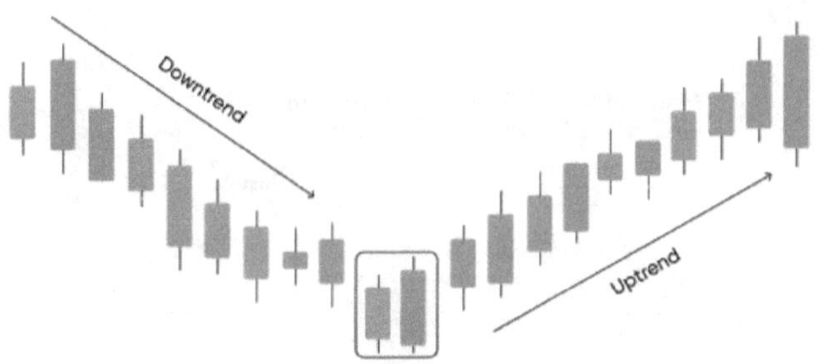

INDIA VIX — FEAR AND MARKET PSYCHOLOGY (DEEP DIVE)

VIX is not just a number; it reflects the entire market's psychology.

When VIX stays low, everyone believes the market is completely under control. But in reality, this is often when big moves are created, because the market becomes overly confident (complacent).

Example:
VIX = 11 → Market is calm → Everyone is confident → Sudden news → Sharp market fall

Conclusion:
When VIX is low, it is better to wait instead of becoming overly aggressive.

NIFTY & VIX INVERSE RELATION

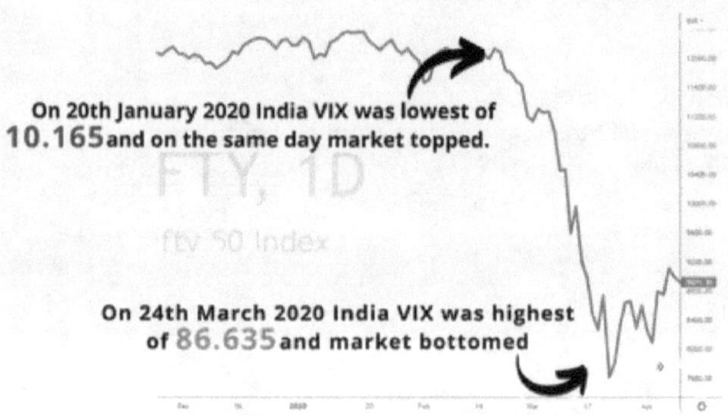

*Images in this book are used from internet sources for reference only.

VIX Behaviour Cycle

VIX generally follows a specific cycle:

Low → Spike → High → Calm

Important Concept:
The biggest market moves usually happen when VIX starts rising from a low level (the transition phase).

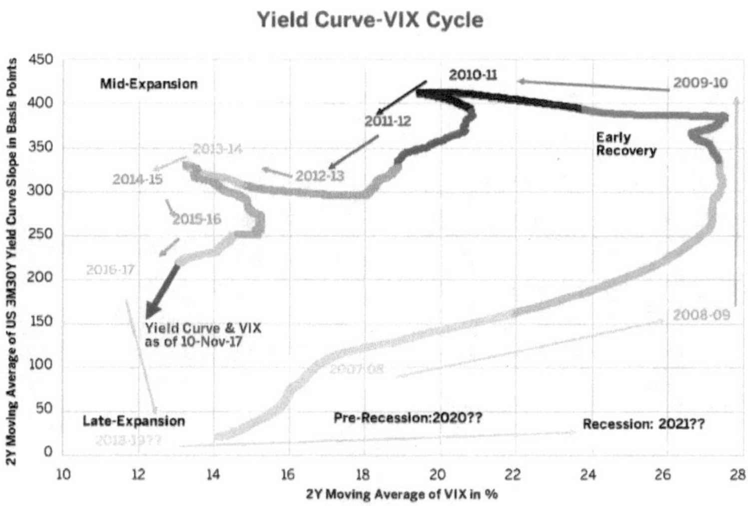

*This image is used from internet sources for reference only.

Impact of the American Market (US Market Impact)

The Indian market is directly influenced by the American market because global fund flows are mainly American-based.

Example:
Dow Jones -2% → The next day, Nifty opens gap down.

Deeper Understanding:
The gap is not important; continuation (sustaining the trend) is more important.

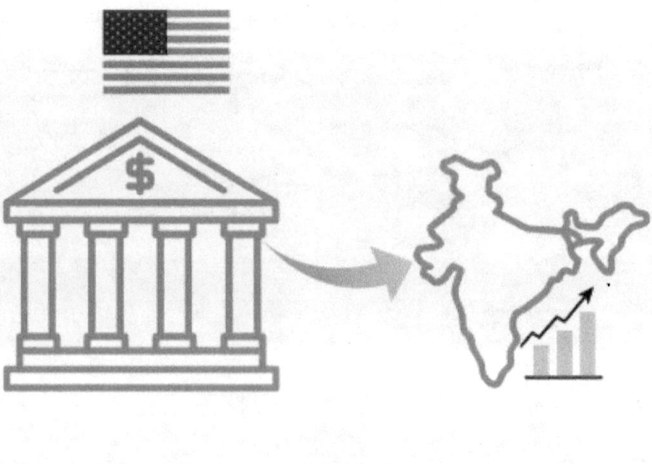

Nasdaq vs Dow — Sector-Based Analysis

Nasdaq → Technology (Tech)-driven
Dow → Stable and defensive

Explanation:

- If the Nasdaq is strong → the IT sector is strong.
- If the Dow is weak → global market sentiment is weak.

Conclusion:
Always make sector-based trading and investment plans.

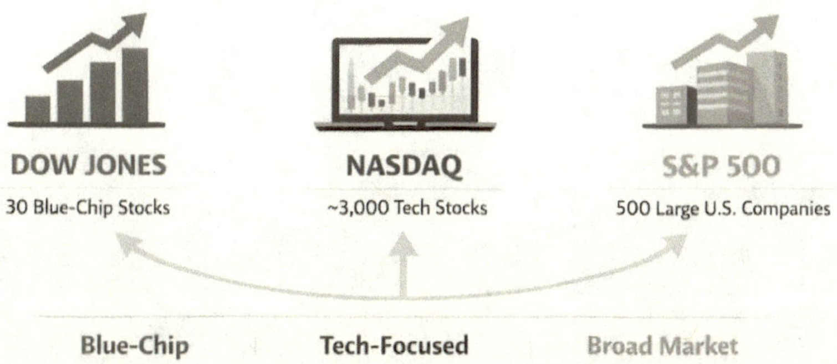

*Images in this book are used from internet sources for reference only.

FED Rate Psychology and the Liquidity Effect

When the FED raises interest rates, it does not only change borrowing costs—it also reduces liquidity from the market (liquidity squeeze).

Example:
Rumors of a rate hike → the market starts falling even before the official announcement.

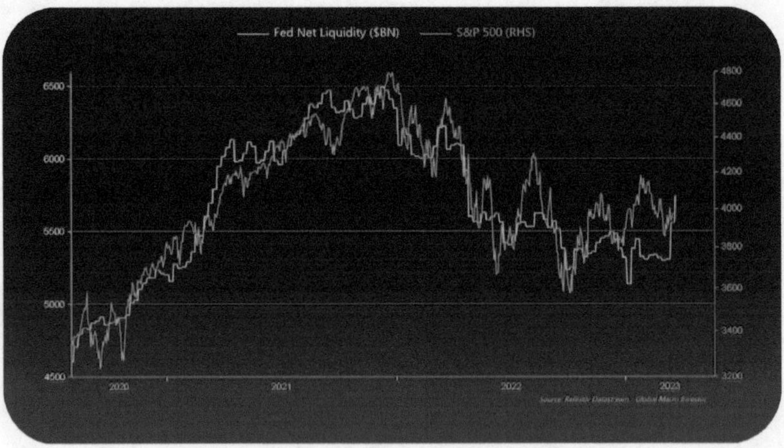

*Images in this book are used from internet sources for reference only.

RBI vs FED — Global and Local Impact

RBI → Focuses on the local economy
FED → Controls the global economy

Insight:
If the FED becomes strict while the RBI remains accommodative → there may be a short-term bounce, but long-term pressure will remain.

Conclusion:
Always follow the global bias first.

*This image is used from internet sources for reference only.

Real Market Framework

Before taking a trade, follow these steps:

1. Check the US market close
2. Watch the SGX Nifty indication
3. Analyze the VIX level
4. Understand the news context

Then take the trade.

Result:
This reduces emotional trading.

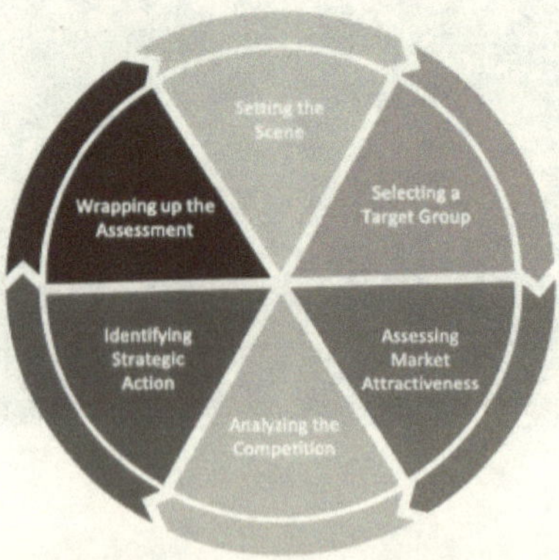

*This image is used from internet sources for reference only.

Identifying a Market Trap

The biggest trap is created when:

- The US market is positive
- The Indian market opens gap up
- VIX is rising

This means hidden selling is going on.

Decision:
Avoid breakout buying during this time.

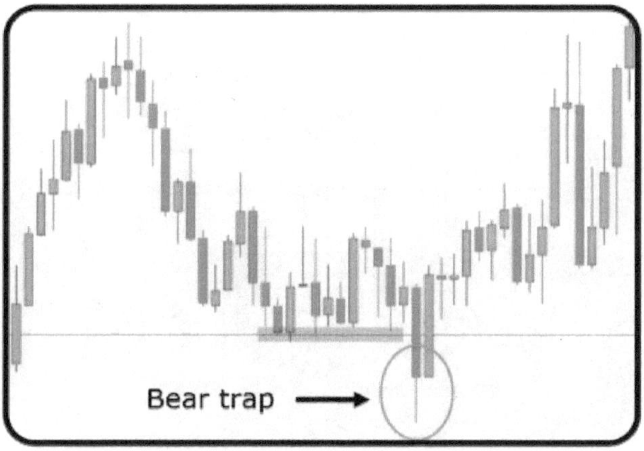

*This image is used from internet sources for reference only.

Intraday Trading Application

Morning:
Check market alignment.

Midday:
Observe changes in the VIX.

Closing:
Verify market strength.

These 3 steps greatly improve accuracy.

*This image is used from internet sources for reference only.

THE CORE PRINCIPLES OF MAKING TRADING DECISIONS

The market never moves randomly.

It moves based on three core forces:

- Liquidity
- Fear
- Expectation

If you understand these three, charts become secondary.

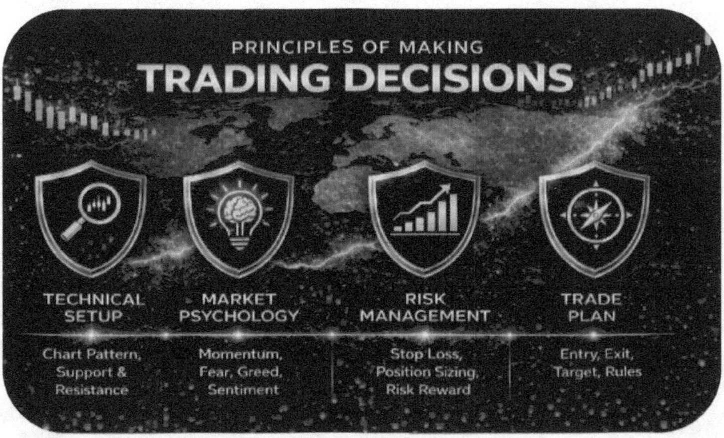

*This image is used from internet sources for reference only.

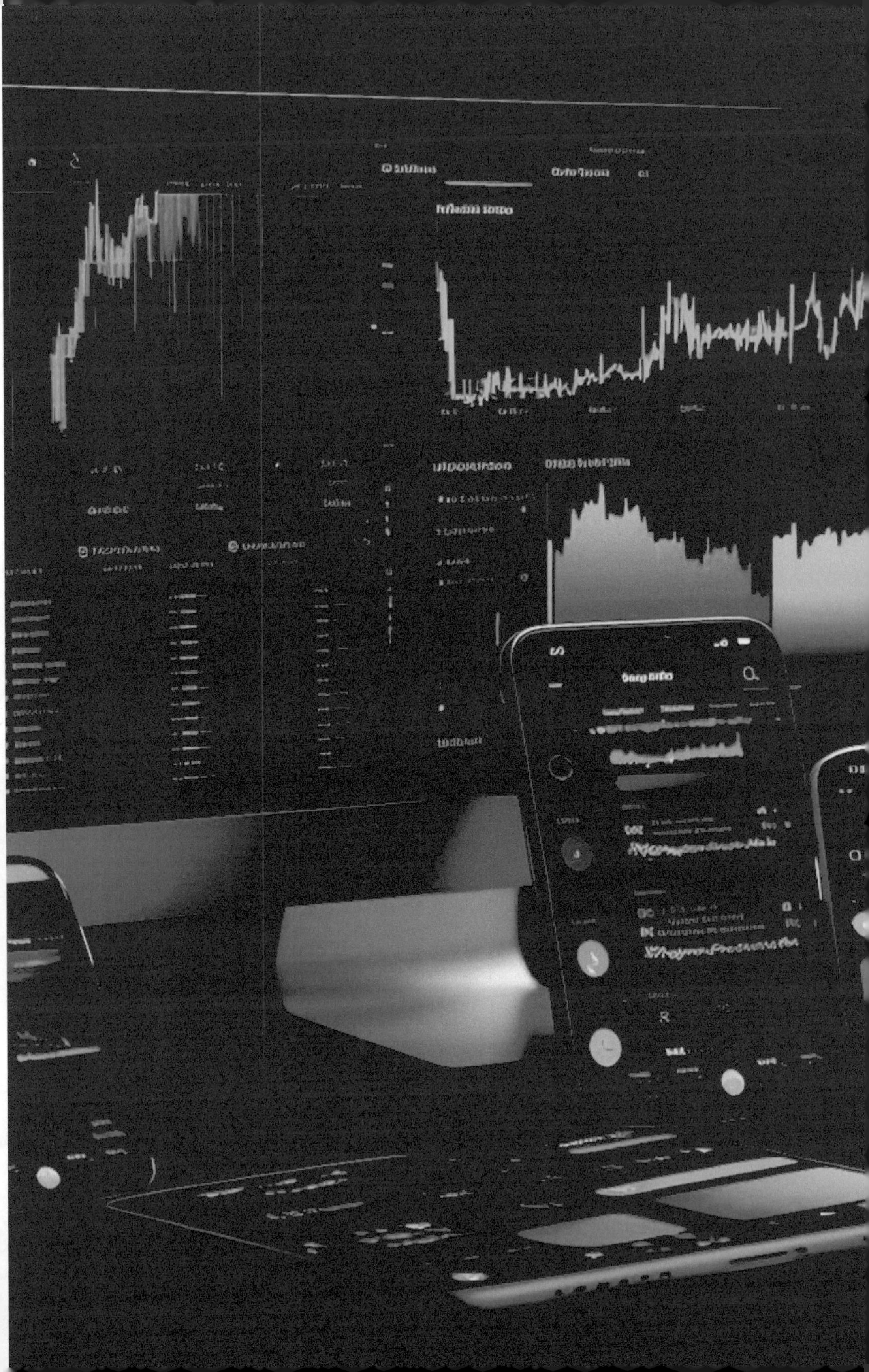

PART 11

Special Chapter:

Advanced Execution Framework (Unique Edition)

What do the people who survive in the market do differently?

Introduction:

Everyone has analysis, but not everyone has execution

Charts are now in everyone's hands.
Indicators are available to everyone.
Everyone sees the patterns.

Yet why do 90% of people still struggle?
Because in the market, profit comes less from prediction and more from execution asymmetry.
In other words, everyone sees the same thing, but not everyone reacts in the same way.

CHAPTER 1

There's an Edge in the Second Move, Not the First Move

Beginners rush into the first candle.
Professionals wait for the reaction.
Why?

The first move can be emotion-driven.
The second move reveals whether the first move was real or just a trap.

Example

At 9:15, Nifty moved sharply upward.
Retail traders rushed to buy.
By 9:25, the price failed to hold.

Here, it became clear that the first move was enthusiasm, not conviction.

Rule

The first move grabs attention; the second move tells the truth.

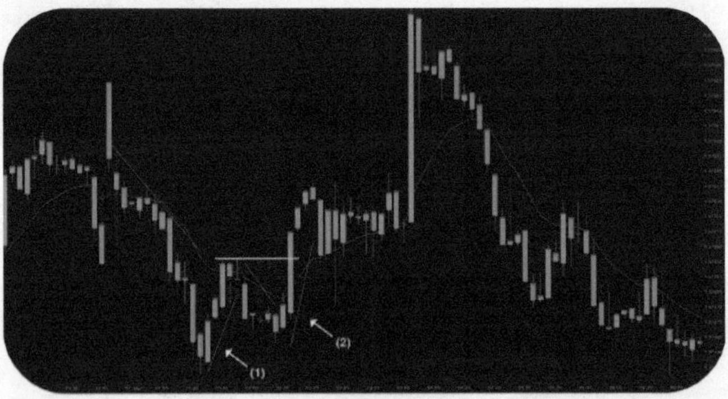

CHAPTER 2

Why Visible Stop Loss Zones Get Hit Again and Again

Everyone places their stop loss at swing lows/highs.
The market knows where the crowd is likely to be wrong.
As a result, visible zones get swept first, and only then does the real move happen.

Practical Insight
Place your stop loss where your trading idea becomes invalid — not at the crowd's obvious levels.

Example
If you place your stop loss just below a support level, the chance of a sweep is high.
A structure break with acceptance gives a stronger invalidation signal.

CHAPTER 3

An entry becomes powerful only when the risk is small but the upside is big.

A good trade does not mean a high win rate.
A good trade means asymmetry.

Example

- Risk: ₹1,000
- Potential Profit: ₹4,000

Even with a 40% win rate, you can still be profitable.

Lesson

Don't look for perfect accuracy — look for favorable skew.

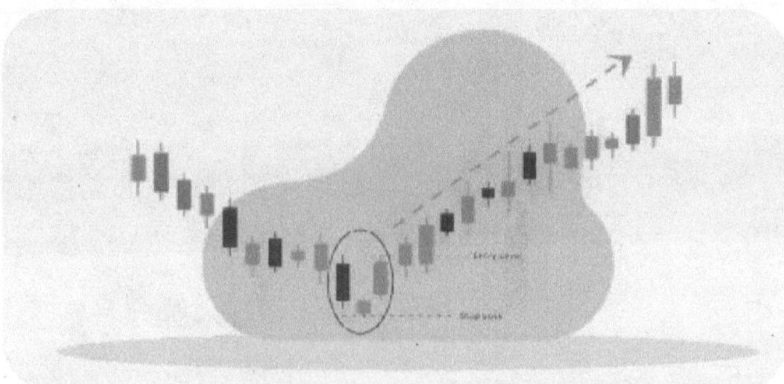

CHAPTER 4

Protecting Daily Profit Is Also Risk Management

Many people think capital protection means only stopping losses.
But if you don't protect your earned profit, a positive day can still turn negative.

Rule
When the daily target is hit, reduce your position size.
Don't let ego turn a green day into a red one.

Example
+₹6,000 profit after 2 trades.
Third revenge/confidence trade → total swing becomes -₹8,000.

CHAPTER 5

No Trade is Also an Execution Decision

The most undervalued skill = knowing when to skip.

When not to take a trade:

- Mixed signals
- Event risk
- Low liquidity
- Emotional state unstable
- Late move already stretched

Truth

Some days, the market gives money.
Some days, the market tests discipline.

CHAPTER 6

Entry Price Isn't Important, Entry Location Is

Whether you enter at ₹100 or ₹101 is not a big deal.
What matters is where you are entering.

Bad Location

- Middle of the range
- Chasing a late breakout
- Random candle

Strong Location

- Retest hold
- Failure reversal zone
- Compression release area

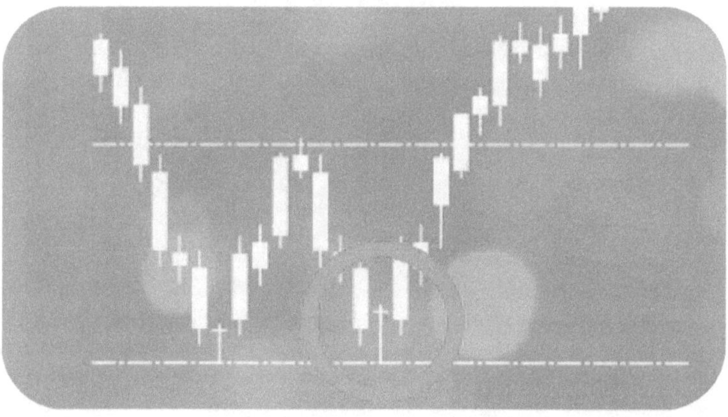

*This image is used from internet sources for reference only.

CHAPTER 7

Scale In, Not All In

Even in a high-conviction trade, never enter with full size at once.

Example
- 30% size as a starter
- Add on confirmation
- Final add when the trend holds

Benefit
- If you're wrong, the damage is smaller.
- If you're right, you still get full participation.

*This image is used from internet sources for reference only.

CHAPTER 8

Exit Shouldn't Be Only Target-Based, It Should Be Information-Based

When new data arrives, the old plan must change.

Example

The trade is in profit.
Suddenly, VIX spikes and the sector shows weakness.
Even if the chart target has not been hit, exiting the trade can still be rational.

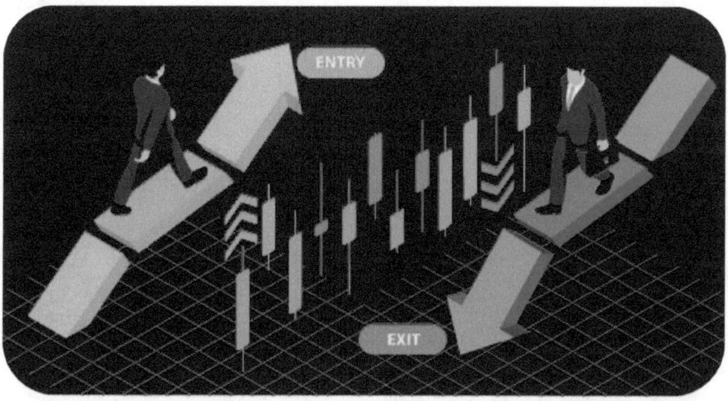

CHAPTER 9

Losing Streak Protocol

Three consecutive losses do not always mean strategy failure.
Maybe the market regime has changed, or you are emotionally tilted.

Protocol

- Reduce position size by half
- Take fewer trades
- Observe more
- Review your last trades

CHAPTER 10

Execution Pyramid

State of Mind
↓
Market Context
↓
Risk Plan
↓
Entry Quality
↓
Exit Discipline
If the bottom isn't right, the top won't hold.
🖋 Final Wisdom
In the market, you don't need to be the smartest —
you need to be repeatable.

CHAPTER 12

SPECIAL CHAPTER:
Real Market Case Studies (Unique Edition)

Where the crowd gets trapped, and where Smart Money operates.

Case 1: Using a Gap Up as Exit Liquidity

Situation

Strong global cues.
The market opens with a gap up.
Retail traders think: "The rally has started."

But some large participants may use the gap up to unload their previous holdings.

How to Identify It?

- Open equals high, with no further progress
- Every bounce gets sold
- Leading stocks remain weak despite a green index

Lesson

Not every gap is demand.
Some gaps are distribution windows.

A Breakout That Buyers Wanted, but Found Only Spectators

Situation

Resistance broke.
The chart looked beautiful. Everyone was excited.
But after the breakout, the price moved sideways and went dead.

Meaning

New buyers did not come in with enough quantity.
The price broke out, but the auction could not continue.

Insight

Breaking the breakout line is not the real signal.
Post-breakout acceptance is the signal.

Case 3: A Violent Fall, but Selling Was Finished

Situation

A sharp fall happened on panic news.
Everyone expected an even bigger crash.
But the candle spread was large, and afterward there was no further downside progress.

Meaning

Heavy selling had already happened.
New sellers were exhausted.

What Pros Watch

Price falling less despite bad sentiment = hidden absorption.

Case 4: Strong Trend, Wrong Trader
(Strong Trend, Wrong Trader)

Situation
The market trend is clearly upward.
The trader keeps shorting because it feels "too high."

Mistake
Price is not expensive — the perception is expensive.
During a strong trend, reversal trades driven by ego are dangerous.

Lesson
Trading against the trend is not intelligence; it is stubbornness.

Case 5: Refusing a Small Loss Creates a Big Loss
(Refusing a small loss creates a big loss)

Situation
Planned stop loss: ₹1,000.
The trader thought, "It will come back."
Loss became ₹7,000.

Deep Truth
The chart did not create the big loss — hope did.

Case 6: Refusing a Small Loss Creates a Big Loss
(Small Loss Refused, Big Loss Created)

Situation
The whole day moved in a boring narrow range.
Retail traders left.
In the closing hour, a sharp expansion came.

Meaning
Low volatility is often a preparation phase.

Lesson
A boring market is not useless.
Often, it is an energy storage zone.

Case 7: News Positive, Price Negative
(News Positive, Price Negative)

Situation
Good results were announced.
But the stock price fell.
Why?
Because the good news was already priced in.
Late buyers got trapped.

Lesson
News is not absolute.
Expectation vs Reality matters.

Case 8: Same Setup, Different Outcome

The same pattern gave two different results in two days. Why?
Because the pattern is constant, but the context is variable.
Context Variables

- Index mood
- VIX
- Sector flow
- Time of day
- Positioning

Reader Edge Formula
Setup + Context + Behaviour = Edge
Setup Alone = Noise

Practical 30-Day Challenge

- Don't just mark setups — write the context as well.
- Before every trade, write your invalidation level.
- After 3 losses, reduce your position size.
- Don't trade blindly on gap openings.
- Review one mistake every week.

Final Wisdom

The crowd enters by looking at patterns,
Professionals enter by looking at reactions.

FINAL WORDS

The first volume will help you understand the market.
The second volume will teach you how to operate in the market with greater maturity.
This is not just a sequel — it is the next-level journey.

Volume 2... Coming Soon.

AUTHOR'S FINAL WORDS TO THE READER

The fact that this book has reached your hands means you are ready to walk the path of learning. And that is the most important thing. Because success in the market begins with interest, then discipline, and finally experience.

I do not want you to read this book and dream of conquering the market overnight. I want you to learn to respect the market. Learn to understand when there is an opportunity, when to wait, when you are wrong, and when you need to stop yourself.

Just as profit is a teacher, loss is also a teacher. The only difference is who learns and who complains. If you learn from every mistake, then no loss will ever go to waste. Remember, big capital is not always the greatest strength. Clear thinking, risk control, patience, and consistency—these are the true companions of the long journey.

If this book can bring even a small change in the way you think, if it makes you pause and think one more time before taking a trade, if you use logic instead of emotion—then my writing has been successful.

This is not the end. This is the beginning. I am with you on your journey of learning. —

Bholanath Das

SELECTED REFERENCES FOR STUDENTS

The journey of learning the stock market never ends in a single day. A book can show the way, but continuous learning makes you stronger. For those who want to go deeper, some selected references are provided below.

Books

1. **The Intelligent Investor** — by Benjamin Graham
The foundation of value investing, margin of safety, and disciplined thinking.

2. **Common Stocks and Uncommon Profits** — by Philip Fisher
Helps in identifying quality businesses.

3. **One Up On Wall Street** — by Peter Lynch
Explains how ordinary people can invest using common sense.

4. **Market Wizards** — by Jack D. Schwager
Covers the mindset and execution philosophy of various successful traders.

SOURCE OF LEARNING / LEARNING SOURCE

- National Stock Exchange of India
- Bombay Stock Exchange
- Securities and Exchange Board of India Investor Education
- Reserve Bank of India Publications
- Company Annual Reports
- Investor Presentations

HOW TO READ THIS

- Don't just memorize quotes.
- Compare the ideas.
- Write notes in your own journal.
- Match them with the real market.
- Don't do blind copying — practice adapted learning.

Contact & Organization Information

About the Organization

School of Day Traders

is a research-based stock market training institute
where real-world experience, market psychology, and
practical trading knowledge are taught together.

Our Mission

Our goal is not just to teach trading,
but to build aware and self-reliant traders—
who can understand the market and make informed decisions.

Contact Us

Phone / WhatsApp: +91 8918082064, +91 83919 39470

Final Words

"Success in the market is not a shortcut;
it is the result of patience, knowledge, and the right decisions."

About the Author

Bholanath Das

NISM Certified Research Analyst (Under SEBI)
Educator | TEDx Speaker
Founder & Research Head - School of Day Traders

www.ingramcontent.com/pod-product-compliance
Lightning Source LLC
LaVergne TN
LVHW100311210926
848480LV00003B/1095

* 9 7 9 8 9 0 5 6 0 1 5 3 8 *